D0375025

COMMITTED

COMMITTED

Men Tell Stories of Love, Commitment, and Marriage

Edited by Chris Knutsen and David Kuhn

BLOOMSBURY

Published by Bloomsbury Publishing, New York and London
Distributed to the trade by Holtzbrinck Publishers

All papers used by Bloomsbury Publishing are natural, recyclable
products made from wood grown in well-managed forests.
The manufacturing processes conform to the environmental
regulations of the country of origin.

Library of Congress Cataloging-in-Publication Data

Committed: men tell stories of love, commitment, and marriage / edited by Chris
Knutsen and David Kuhn.—1st U.S. ed.
p. cm.
ISBN 1-58234-499-X (hc)
1. American prose literature—Male authors. 2. Male authors, American—Biography.
3. Man-woman relationships. 4. Commitment (Psychology).
5. Marriage. I. Knutsen, Chris. II. Kuhn, David.

PS648.M28C66 2005
818'.5080803543—dc22
2004016183

First U.S. Edition 2005

1 3 5 7 9 10 8 6 4 2

Typeset by Hewer Text Ltd, Edinburgh
Printed in the United States of America
by Quebecor World Fairfield

CONTENTS

Preface: Number Four

JAY MCINERNEY

Let me put my credentials right up front: I have been married three times, which would seem to qualify me to introduce and pass preliminary judgment on a book about commitment from the male point of view, even as it would seem to make me a prime candidate for the kind of instruction and inspiration presumably enshrined herein. Samuel Johnson famously remarked that marriage is the triumph of hope over experience—an observation more appropriate to second and third marriages. I prefer to think of myself as an incurable romantic rather than a three-time loser.

This past month, I was supposed to get married for the fourth time. Jeanine and I have been together off and on for some five year now. We had booked the church overlooking the harbor of Gustavia in St. Barth's, bought the plane tickets, invited the guests, talked to the minister, and engaged the services of a caterer. The projected wedding was to have taken place more than a year after the proposal, in part to accommodate the demands of my work, and in part, perhaps, to give my feet a chance to get warmer. I was in the middle of writing a novel and it seemed important to me to have it finished before I embarked on another matrimonial voyage. I can admit now that I was not unhappy at the prospect of a long engagement, comforted to have an excuse to put the date off into a somewhat distant future. (I actually considered following up the current novel with a comic novella about a writer who finds himself

1

unable to finish a book after telling his girlfriend that he'll marry her as soon as he finishes his book.)

Last Thanksgiving, with the novel and the relationship bogging down more than somewhat, my fiancée called the wedding off. Or rather, she postponed it indefinitely. Our relationship improved almost immediately. We are, I would say, deeply committed to each other, living together, going on vacations with my third ex-wife and my two kids, walking our French bulldog and boldly planning a future together. And we have both been trying to figure out what it all means for the past few months.

There are, it always seemed to me, two frames of mind in which one should approach marriage: either to be compelled beyond reason, or to be fully cognizant of one's motives. Or so I thought until I read the essays in this book. "There's a lot to be said for acting impetuously when you're young," David Owen proposes, in defense of becoming a groom at the tender age of twenty-three. "Clueless people are more likely to be smart by accident than on purpose, so why not roll the dice." Owen's gamble seems to have paid off nicely over the ensuing decades. In his essay "Companion Species," Rick Moody describes how he gradually and grudgingly realized, over the course of a decade, that he was for all intents and purposes *in* a marriage—that in learning not to hate his girlfriend's cats he had unwittingly overcome his fear of commitment. Chip Brown, on the other hand, seems to have precipitously proposed for the first time at the ripe age of forty-three and then to have spent a great deal of time trying to figure out why he waited so long—only to conclude that his destiny finally called him to the altar when it was ready.

The reaction to the postponement of our nuptials was largely bifurcated along gender lines. Despite her protestations that it was her own idea and that she stood by it, Jeanine's girlfriends treated her like a victim, or possibly a fool. "The first reaction was, I'm so sorry, you poor thing. When I told them it was my decision they thought I was mad. It was like I set my trap, I lured and caught my prey and then inexplicably let him get away. It was like I bought a vineyard and then suddenly decided to stop drinking." Jeanine's girlfriends are, almost without exception, sophisticated Manhattan professional women in their thirties and forties. They have, presumably imbibed the tenets of feminism with their mother's milk, or baby formula. They've watched *Sex and the City*. In fact, one of them, Candace Bushnell, is the author of the book—that smart, cynical bible of feisty urban single girldom. Candace, who got married a couple of years ago, was among those who seemed to feel that Jeanine's catch-and-release strategy was incredibly misguided.

Whereas some of my male friends, most of whom consider Jeanine a very attractive and desirable partner, "a stone babe," as one put it, whom I was lucky to be sharing a bed with, were pretty much of the opinion that I had dodged a bullet. This reaction may have been specific to my own circumstances; after all, as one of them said, "Your track record is not exactly inspiring." But more than that, I think, they were vicariously and perhaps theatrically giving voice to that putative male instinct which basically translates as a fear of commitment—a point of view hyperbolically represented here by Andy Borowitz, who compares marriage to death and taxes and suggests that "no man loses his bachelor status without profound suffering—emotional, mental, and even physical . . ."

This idea that men are reluctant settlers, biologically programmed to spread their seed across the savanna, takes a bit of a beating from many of the other contributors. What is most remarkable and possibly inspiring about the essays here is the way that most of them, if sometimes by circuitous routes, eventually deconstruct this stereotype of male commitment aversion (not to mention the stereotype about men being emotionally inarticulate). If the husbands and lovers in this book feel constrained, they are, like the narrator in Dylan Thomas's "Fern Hill"—singing in their chains, like the sea. "Getting married actually felt like nothing else so much as a liberation," says Geoff Dyer, who got married shortly after taking his new girlfriend to the Burning Man Festival. David Grand, after recounting his hair-raising dating history, sounds a similar note. "With Christine in my life I have been granted the freedom to learn what it means to be a man." And John Burnham Schwartz credits his wife with nothing less than saving his sanity.

"Each marriage is a country unto itself," James Wolcott suggests, "with its own lingo, customs, unwritten regulations, secret passwords, telepathic powers, and historical landmarks." And indeed one of the pleasures of this collection is a voyeuristic one—the opportunity to experience a guided tour behind the bedroom doors of nearly two dozen sovereign and independent marriages, no two of which seem very much alike. In an essay in which he turns the lancing of a hideous boil into a profoundly romantic gesture, David Sedaris implicitly reminds us that commitment is an emotional rather than a legal concept. Unlike David Sedaris and his partner, I have the legal option to formalize my commitment to Jeanine in all states of the union—although a rational state might erect higher hurdles for people like me who have over-exercised the option. But I like to think that, at this relatively late date, I am still learning the joys and responsibilities of commitment, and I am strangely optimistic about the future—the more so after reading this book.

Of Course

GEOFF DYER

I'd only known my girlfriend for a fortnight when I popped the question. I say *girlfriend* but that puts it too strongly; we could have been in the midst of a series of brief encounters. For the sake of complete accuracy, then, I told Rebecca, the woman I had recently started sleeping with, that I had a *very important*—in fact a *life-determining*—*question* to ask her.

"So can I ask you?" I said.

"Yes."

"Okay. Ready?"

"Yes."

"Do you want to go to Burning Man with me?"

This was in June 2000. Burning Man, the annual freak-out in the Black Rock Desert, takes place in the week leading up to the Labor Day weekend, but because we would be coming from England and because Rebecca, at that time, had a senior job in publishing and because going to Burning Man is a huge palaver and involves months of planning and commitment, we needed to get on the case immediately. She didn't hesitate.

"Of course," she said. It was one of the great *of courses* of all time because although I had talked about Burning Man pretty well nonstop from the moment we met, although I always turned every other topic of conversation round to Burning Man and was interested in almost nothing *but* Burning Man, Rebecca, prior to meeting me, had not been part of any of the scenes that bring Europeans within the gravitational tug of Black Rock City. She'd never been a raver, wasn't part of the international trance scene, and wasn't even into nightclubbing in London.

The very short version of what resulted from that "of course" is as follows: we went to Burning Man and, within a few days of getting back, arranged to get married as soon as bureaucratically possible (October 12, 2000).

We didn't want to wait and I'm glad we didn't because I hate waiting. I am temperamentally incapable of waiting. Waiting for me is torture. I've spent too much of my life waiting and I can't wait another second for *anything*, but in this context—the context of the narrative of how we couldn't and didn't wait to get married—it's necessary, well, not to *wait* exactly but at least go right back to the beginning, to the night we met.

It was at a party thrown by the art magazine *Modern Painters*, at the Lisson Gallery, for the launch of the new issue to which I had contributed an evangelical piece about the art of Burning Man. It was a nice party with a relaxed vibe. By this I mean that in addition to the expected bottles of red and white wine, there was a huge and varied quantity of beer. There was such an endless flow of beer that thirsty guests could relax in the knowledge that it was not going to run out. I was also relaxed because I wasn't looking for a girlfriend. I wasn't dating anyone at the time but I wasn't exuding the off-putting air of celibate desperation that has often sabotaged my attempts to get a girlfriend and which has, in turn, made me even more desperate to get one. I was, as they say in the submarine world, at periscope depth. Although I wasn't looking for a girl-friend, I three-sixty-ed the room, had a look around to reassure myself that there really were no gorgeous women here and that I could concentrate on doing what I had come to do, which was to drink a lot of free beer. That's what I was looking forward to doing: having a serious drink. It was going to be one of those great nights of freeloading when you go out, have a skinful, get back home, and think, *Great—I've drunk up a storm, had an absolute skinful, and haven't spent a penny*! But then, as I scanned the room, beer in hand, already looking forward to following up that first beer with a second, third, and probably an eighth and ninth, I realized that it was one of those parties where there are *lots* of attractive women. A kind of rule is at work here. If there is one attractive woman at a party, that means there will probably be several more—and if there are lots of attractive women, that means there will be one in particular who is *very* attractive. In this case she had long, dark hair, had eyes like the Madonna, was tall, thin, and was not smoking cigarettes. If she had been smoking cigarettes, the spell would have been broken and I would have concentrated on swilling huge quantities of beer, drinking up a storm and going home without having spent a penny. But this beautiful woman with long hair and eyes like the Madonna was not smoking. She was wearing stylish London clothes. I don't really know about these things. Especially back then, before I married the woman wearing them, I didn't. At that stage, it was funky trance-wear that caught my eye, but she still looked nice in her modest and expensive-looking London anti-trance-wear. I established all of this on a number of sweeps through the room, but there was never any chance to speak with her because she was always speaking with someone else, and although I was introduced to many people in the early stages of the evening and often hovered in her vicinity, hoping to be introduced by virtue of geographical proximity, it never quite happened. During one of these protracted hovers she did glance over at me, though, and this was all the enticement and incitement I needed to speak to her even though we had not been introduced.

"Have we met before?" I said.

"No, but I know who you are," she replied courteously.

To which I replied, in my mock-pompous way, "Geoff Dyer, of course."

"Rebecca Wilson," she said. We shook hands. She was there with a bespectacled guy called Mark who didn't know I was doing my mock-pompous thing. He thought I was just doing my pompous thing. As a result, I learned subsequently, he thought I was "somewhat of an asshole." I also learned that, as I had been hovering and generally waiting for a chance to speak to her, Rebecca had said to Mark that she fancied me. To which Mark, who is gay and from Maryland, had said, "You don't want to bother with a skinny, gray-haired old thing like that!" It was a fine example of the myriad blessings of heterosexuality. From this admittedly small sample we conclude that I had reached the age where I was no longer attractive to men (if I ever had been) but was still attractive to women. It's even possible that although I was in undoubted physical decline, I was more attractive to women than I used to be because I was no longer giving off the desperate air that had been a feature of my life throughout my twenties and, if we are being utterly frank, much of my thirties. The lack of desperation manifested itself in my being comfortable about an inability, as we say in England, to "chat up" women. I had never been able to do this but I had only recently given up trying to, and even if I was, at some level, trying to do exactly that, it didn't feel like *chatting up* a beautiful woman with eyes like the Madonna; it felt like chatting to a nice, clever person who happened to be beautiful. I slightly worry about this in retrospect. Rebecca has a tendency to get cornered by bores at parties. People blah on at her because she is such a good listener. I wonder if I blahed on. And if I did blah on, what did I blah on about? Myself, probably, and Burning Man. It is also possible that an overeagerness to appear intelligent manifested itself in a tendency to express vehement opinions, of a generally negative bent. In practice this meant I *denounced* people, especially internationally successful authors with high and, in my view, undeserved reputations. To compensate I exaggerated the achievements of underrated writers such as myself whose work deserved a far larger audience.

We could easily have become deadlocked in this, but I happened to mention a terrific novel I had just read, published by the company Rebecca worked for, called *Reservation Road* by John Burnham Schwartz. And not only did Rebecca share my high opinion of this book, but she was actually Schwartz's editor. She had *acquired* the book. Yippee! We were in agreement and we were chatting away like mad, having a good old chat, creating positive vibrations and everything, and although I didn't know that Mark was gay, I was starting to sense that he was just a friend rather than a boyfriend and that he was no longer thinking I was *somewhat of an asshole*. I was right about this: by the end of the evening, Rebecca told me later, he thought I was a *total* asshole.

Although we had been having a good old chat Rebecca said she had to be leaving. There was no need to ask for her phone number. I knew she worked for Weidenfeld and Nicolson and "perhaps," I said, "perhaps I could call you there."

"You know where I am," she said. In a way I was relieved that she left when she did because although I had enjoyed speaking with her, I had been somewhat on my best behavior, and now that she had gone I could start drinking up a storm and having the skinful that I had refrained from having during our stimulating chat.

I called her on Tuesday—which, she later told me, was exactly when she thought I would call if I was going to call (which she knew I would). I was forty-two at the time and in some ways I was quite wise, wise enough to know that it is no good trying to set up a romantic encounter with someone in publishing in the guise of a semiprofessional meeting (a lunch, say, to talk about forthcoming books). So I phrased my question carefully.

"I'd love to see you one evening," I said, emphasizing but not quite italicizing the *love*. "If that's possible," I added after a telling pause.

"Yes," she said, and then, after an equally telling pause, "that's

9

possible." The reply was every bit as clever as my question and similarly encoded. By saying "that's possible" she was also intimating that *anything* was possible. There then followed the part of the conversation I had been dreading, so totally dreading, in fact, that I'd eventually phoned without even being sure how to address it. This was the problem of what to do on our first date. The worst thing you can do on a first date is to do what people nearly always do on a first date: go out to dinner. I couldn't face that, couldn't face any aspect of it. I couldn't face the tacit compatibility check of the whole evening and I couldn't face the look of disappointment on her face when I suggested—as I knew I shouldn't, as I was determined not to, but as I knew I would—either that we split the bill or that she pick up the tab and claim it back on expenses. Anything was better than that, than going out to dinner and running through the list of who likes what, but I wasn't sure what to do instead. I was in the twilight of my raving years, and ideally, if it had been completely up to me, we'd have gone out dancing and necked a bunch of pills. The other possibility, one that I hesitated broaching, was that she came down to visit me at my flat in Brighton on the south coast. Although I kept a room in a flat in London, I mainly lived in Brighton, in the greatest apartment I will ever own. It was on the fourth and fifth floors of a building on First Avenue, I said. The top floor was one big chill-out room. One whole wall of this room was a window with doors leading out onto the epic terrace. If it was sunny, the distinction between indoors and outdoors dissolved, I said. We discussed various possibilities about what to do, but since Rebecca was busy until Saturday, and since people from London always like to visit Brighton, and since I had talked up my flat so much, I said, "How about coming down to Brighton on Saturday?" And she said yes.

Saturday was gray and cold, but did I care? Yes, I cared. I was pissed off. I was really pissed off. I had foreseen a day out on my terrace with the sun beating down, drinking fresh fruit juices and hanging out as though we were in South Beach or L.A. Instead, I was looking out at the grayness pressing against the window. Then the phone rang. It was Rebecca. As soon as I heard her voice, I knew she had got cold feet and was calling to cancel, but, no, it was just that she had missed her train and was going to be late.

I went to the station to meet her. Her hair was long and lovely. She was wearing a loose-fitting Japanese shirt, and in keeping with this oriental touch, we greeted each other by pressing the palms of our hands together and bowing—something I'd been affecting since going to Thailand earlier in the year and which she had picked up from spending time in India. It was a nice beginning, ironic and genuine in equal measure without being genuine—or ironic—at all.

"I'm so sorry I'm late," she said, looking and sounding really quite mortified.

"That's okay," I said.

"I hate being late."

"Me too," I said. "I mean it doesn't matter that you were late today but in general I deplore lateness."

"Me too!"

"I love punctuality so much. I'm not meaning to reproach you but I do love it."

"I love it too!" she insisted.

"Then why were you late?" I pleaded.

"Have I spoiled everything?"

"Yes. The day is ruined."

"Shall I just go straight back to London?"

"Shall we have a coffee and talk about it?" I said. "See if we can salvage something from a day that has already been comprehensively ruined?"

"I'd like to try."

This conversation pretty much set the tone for our entire subsequent relationship. We've spent hundreds of evenings since then, talking bollocks like this ("talking the nonsense," we call it) about one thing or another, but, at the same, we were being quite honest: the fact that we are both so uptight about punctuality makes us feel totally relaxed together.

From the station we went to a café, where we ordered two cappuccinos "*without* chocolate on the top" and sent them back because they arrived *with* chocolate on the top. Even when they were remade, minus the offending chocolate, the cappuccinos weren't up to much, and we had a frank discussion about cappuccinos in general and I blathed on about the cappuccino situation in Brighton in particular. With our cappuccinos we each had a croissant. I say *croissant* but really they were just dreary croissant-shaped buns. I put raspberry jam on mine, to liven it up a bit. After that we walked down to the depressing seafront. Brighton is a depressing place. It's especially depressing if the weather's bad, and it's even more depressing if it's gray in June when it's meant to be sunny and blue and you have just drunk the kind of scalding bucket of foam that passes for a cappuccino in these parts. We walked along the promenade and looked out at the sea.

"*Oed' und leer das Meer,*" I said, and then, after a pause: "Wagner. *Tristan und Isolde,* of course. Quoted by T. S. Eliot in *The Waste Land.*"

"You really *are* an asshole aren't you?" said Rebecca. "It's that 'of course' that I really hate."

"I was sort of joking," I said. "Of course."

"I wasn't," she said, slipping her arm into mine.

It started drizzling soon after this, and then, as happens, the drizzle became rain. There was nothing to do except go back to my amazing flat. Rebecca said how much she loved my chill-out room with its lilac walls, UV lights, incense, statues of the Buddha, and its pervasive *I've just got back from Thailand where I did nothing but smoke pot for a month* look. Later she said it was like a cross between a vegetarian café at a festival and a nightclub, but that was only after we were married (but before the divergences in our tastes in interior decoration had resulted in some quite brutal arguments). I made risotto—the one thing I know how to cook well. We ate the risotto upstairs in this huge chill-out room, one wall of which was entirely comprised of windows against which the rain lashed relentlessly.

It was late afternoon. If it had been sunny, the sun, at this time of day, would have been pouring into the room, flooding everything with gold light. Instead, as Rebecca said, it was "like being on a trawler in the North Sea." It was still fun though, especially after we'd had a couple of bong hits. This was a slight gamble: we could have got all weirded out, both by the fact that we were up here in my flat in Brighton and hardly knew each other and by the way the weather was so bad on a day when I had so wanted it to be good. As it happened, the grass made us feel even more relaxed and I stopped getting bummed out about the rain and the lashing wind. We were sitting on the sofa together, listening to Sultan Khan play the Raga Yaman ("strictly speaking, it is of course an early-evening raga," I said). It was fine sitting there, not feeling self-conscious about not speaking, lost in the tidal sob of the sarangi.

When I was younger, I regularly used to try to sleep with women before I really wanted to. I would make passes at them not because I wanted to but because I felt I ought to. If Rebecca and I had gone out to dinner, we would either have had to say good-bye after dinner and drinks or we could have agreed to go home together prematurely. As it was, like this, we could just listen to music and chat about cappuccinos or me or Burning Man until gradually, without any nudging or coaxing, our hands touched and we were kissing.

Rebecca stayed that night and the next. On Monday she had to go to work. I remained in Brighton for the whole of that week and on Friday she came down again.

"You're even more beautiful than I remembered," I said as I opened the door and saw her again.

"I've been wet all week," she said.

We didn't actually go on a date until the week after that, when we went to the launch party for Will Self's new novel in London. It was in Rebecca's flat in London, later that night, that I asked her about Burning Man and she said, "Of course."

I knew we would have a good time there, and I also knew that Burning Man is a parable and test. The previous year I had gone with my then girlfriend and we had known within days that we would split up. I'd kept wishing I was there alone, partly because of all the sexual opportunities that weren't coming my way, but mainly because of the issue of responsibility. I was left doing everything, taking care of our camp, making sure things didn't get blown away, while my girlfriend went running around the *playa* and generally going as crazy as a kid in a sweet shop. We both became total Burning Man converts but we also knew we'd split up. We duly did so the following January, a few days after going to see a film called *Lies* at the ICA. At the time I did not attach any significance to this. That was just the way it happened.

Rebecca and I flew to San Francisco on Friday, August 25. We hired a van, bought a couple of cheap bikes and tons of food and water. There was so much to take care of and sort out in those few days prior to going to Burning Man that what we mainly looked forward to doing once we got there was sleeping.

A slightly strange light was in the sky as Rebecca and I headed north from Reno toward Gerlach late on Tuesday afternoon, the day after the festival had started. It wasn't as bright as it should have been and I had to grip the wheel tightly because our van was being thumped by strong winds. We arrived in Black Rock City after dark and couldn't find the Canadian friends we had arranged to camp with—but we did find our friends from San Francisco. We spent the first night at their camp, sleeping in the back of our van, and the next morning decided to stay put. We also decided not to bother pitching our tent: it was so cold and windy that we were better off continuing to sleep in our van. A good decision, it turned out, since 2000 will be remembered by everyone who went as the year Black Rock City was assailed by terrible winds and dust storms. We spent a lot of time just hunkered down in our friends' yurt or cowering in the back of our van, feeling it buffeted by these gale-force dust storms. We also spent a lot of time *rummaging* in our van. *A place for everything and everything in its place*—that was our motto even if we rarely managed to abide by it. We were always looking for things—a can opener or a pair of socks—which, I insisted in tones of absolute bewilderment, "I had in my hand two seconds earlier." We did other things, fun things, but it's the rummaging I mainly remember—the rummaging and the weather, which had conspired against us on our first day in Brighton and which was conspiring against us on our first time together at Burning Man. To be honest, although it was great being at Burning Man, it was also disappointing. It was windy and dusty and cold. One night it even rained. Our bike tires became so clogged with mud the wheels wouldn't go round and we had to drag them back to camp.

"It's like being at fucking Glastonbury," I whined. The struggle to survive is part of the experience of Burning Man, and I can see how, for people from sunny California, it *is* fun, but as I told anyone who would listen, we *came* from a rainy, windy place with poor visibility and I didn't really need to come all the way to Nevada—to the Nevada *desert*, what's more—to experience more of the same. We had a great time but we could have had a better time, which meant we had a terrible time because I spent all my time thinking how much better it would have been if the weather had been better. I cannot make the best of a bad job, put a brave face on things, or settle for second best. Anything less than the apotheosis of whatever it is I am hoping to experience will be a crushing disappointment. This is an item of faith with me, and although this attitude has been a terrible burden that has, in some ways, blighted my life by making imperfect situations twenty times worse, it has also—as we will shortly see—stood me in good stead in other respects.

From time to time Rebecca has outbreaks of something like herpes around her eyes. She gets these tiny ulcers on the inside of her eyelids and it is agony for her. One morning, soon after we had started sleeping together, she woke up with her left eye swollen shut like a boxer's. It was the saddest thing, especially since her eyes are so lovely. A week after getting back to London from Burning Man, I fell ill. At first I had a sore throat and flu, but within days I was iller than I had ever been in my life. My throat and tongue were covered in thirty or forty white ulcers. I couldn't eat, couldn't swallow, couldn't even get out of bed. My head felt as if it were going to implode and explode at the same time. The doctor said that herpes was the most likely diagnosis. I moped around in Rebecca's flat all day, whimpering and waiting for her to come home with soothing treats—juices, books, CDs—in the evening.

Fortunately we had already done the paperwork for getting married. We were doing it as cheaply as possible. No expense had not been spared. Two days before our wedding I went to a literary prize-giving at the Reform Club, where I ate a lunch that looked as if it had been sitting around since Graham Greene and Anthony Powell had dined there before the war. I'd just gotten over this herpes-type thing and now I had food poisoning. As a result, on the day of our lackluster wedding, I looked like death warmed up. Rebecca looked gorgeous, of course. We didn't invite our parents, just two friends (one of whom was that asshole Mark). We went to the registry office on the bus and came back home on the bus after a lunch that Rebecca was persuaded—after some initial reluctance—

to claim back on expenses. Although I still felt shitty from the food poisoning and the herpes, it didn't matter because we had at least succeeded in getting married as quickly and cheaply as possible.

Aside from its amazing cheapness the only unusual thing about our wedding was an agreement we made—a private addendum to the regular vows—whereby I would be free to write anything I wanted about us and our relationship, irrespective of whether it was true.

Obviously we got married in great haste, but were we *rash* as well as hasty? No, partly because a week at Burning Man is the equivalent of a year of normal life, and partly because this apparent hastiness was actually founded on a long patience. One of the most important qualities in life is to hold out for happiness. I've known plenty of people who were incapable of really holding out for their own happiness. They've made do, settled for the next-best thing, made the best of a less than perfect job. I'd had lots of girlfriends, had even, on occasions, been on the brink of making long-term commitments, but always at some point I was selfish enough to jump ship. Either I would find someone who could be everything to me or I'd continue as I was, quite happily, on the serial monogamy treadmill with its interludes of loneliness, involuntary celibacy, and total despair. In a world with however many millions of women in it, it didn't seem too much to hold out for someone who was beautiful, funny, sexy, clever, kind, punctual, with nice manners and good moral bearing. I mention beautiful first because, for me, that was essential if I was to make any kind of commitment or achieve any kind of relaxation. I *had to have* a beautiful girlfriend. Otherwise, if I went to a party, I'd always be wishing I were with someone more beautiful. Because of this obsession with beauty I'd often had girlfriends who, though beautiful, weren't friends at all. Now I had a *beautiful wife* who was my friend and who was clever and kind and everything else. So getting married actually felt like

17

nothing else so much as a liberation. It didn't feel like settling down—which I've never had any urge to do—and it didn't feel like it required any conscious effort on the part of either Rebecca or me. We can't even remember who asked whom. It was all like a continuation of that first afternoon when we were sitting on the sofa listening to an early-evening raga and the next minute we were kissing—and then we were married.

I've noticed that certain things that happen in life—often the things that are most important—seem to occur without your conscious participation. It's almost as if you are oddly passive, that things just fall into place. Of course you are not completely passive, but whereas life often feels as if you were riding a bike with the brakes on—every attempt at progress is met with some kind of resistance—there are instances when you are scarcely aware of having to exert yourself. Destiny is not handed to you on a plate, but sometimes the effort normally demanded by life is replaced by a feeling of ease and grace. You get it in tennis during those strange interludes when you find yourself making strokes in such a way that the distinction between what you have been trying to do and what you are actually doing evaporates and you are just . . . *playing tennis*. It happens in writing when the words, which have been coming only grudgingly and haltingly, begin to flow. In both circumstances you know that you are doing it right even though you can't say exactly what it is that you're doing differently. This is how getting married felt—like doing something right without being sure why. For me, this was confirmed by a little incident that occurred when we'd been married for a couple of months.

Six months before meeting Rebecca I was in the lingerie department of Fenwick's on Bond Street in London with my then girlfriend (with whom I'd first gone to Burning Man). While she was in the changing room trying on underwear, a woman came into the shop. Tall; beautiful eyes, long hair. I couldn't take my eyes off her. It wasn't just that she was beautiful, she transfixed me totally.

My heart went out to her. There was a smoldering of desire—what kind of underwear was she was buying?—but mainly I felt the familiar melancholy of longing. I sort of fell in love with her then and there but knew I would never see her again. She seemed to be in a hurry. I watched her pay and leave. She didn't see me. End of story.

Time passed. A million other things happened, most of them forgotten. I broke up with my girlfriend around this time and then, six months later, met, fell in love with, and married Rebecca. And then one morning I woke up and realized, immediately and with absolute certainty, that the woman lying next to me, Rebecca, my wife, was the woman I had seen that day in Fenwick's.

After leaving Fenwick's my girlfriend and I had gone to see a Korean S&M film at the ICA . . . I couldn't remember the name of the film but, yes, there it was in my diary for January 22: "Saw *Lies* @ ICA." We'd walked down to Pall Mall in bright afternoon sunlight that ricocheted off the windows of buses and cars. The branches of trees were stark against the blue sky. We arrived at the film with several minutes to spare and killed time in the bookshop. All of which means we must have been in Fenwick's between two and two thirty. Rebecca checked *her* diary. Yes, she had been in Fenwick's that day, at about that time—and she *was* in a rush, her car was parked on a yellow line—buying underwear because, later that day, she was flying off to see her lover in New York.

So it was true: I'd completely forgotten that first glimpse of her— but I had never quite forgotten it. The memory developed as I slept, its colors becoming deeper, more distinct: the ghost of a dream, but permanent, lovely.

The King of Banter

TAD FRIEND

I used to be the king of banter. At parties, I kicked ass, springing into conversations as if judges were at ringside. Banter, like boxing, is a form of ritualized disagreement conducted from a crouch, a display of aggression that from afar looks like grace. To banter well, you have to counter every observation someone makes, or at least deflect it. Jab, jab, jab, stick and move.

A woman asks how you are, you say, "Recovering." The idea is that you are privy to late-night epiphanies, that you greet the dawn with a snarl of triumph.

"From lack of sleep?"

"Nah," you say, "from my own procrastination."

"Is there a twelve-step program for that?" she asks, getting into the rhythm of it.

"Actually, it's more like a thirty-six-step program."

The other secret to banter is the callback, a term from comedy writing. It's basically Chekhov's idea that if you see a gun on the wall in the first act, it has to go off by the third. The woman you're chatting with may believe that she's swarming the flame, but she's just filling your holsters. Maybe she chokes on a canapé and you say, "Need help?" and she, recovering, says, "No, if you can ask for the Heimlich maneuver, you don't need it."

"You can never be too careful . . ." you say, making as if to embrace her, and she laughs, probably. Five minutes later, you

20

mention that you've just published a book, and she says, "Oh, what's it called?"

"*The Heimlich Maneuver*, oddly enough—it's available every-where."

"I don't go into bookstores much—*so* many books. But if I find myself at Barnes and Noble, I'll be sure to ask for it."

"See, if you can ask for it, you don't really need it." And so on. The callback demonstrates that you've been paying close atten-tion, but only in the way that the bass man awaits the piano player's cue to take a solo. Virtuosity can look like intimacy, but not for long.

For many years, I longed for a women who could fire back. I had the idea that I'd find the perfect partner in banter and we'd just stand around being witty, like William Powell and Myrna Loy in *The Thin Man*, only without all the pain-in-the-ass crime solving. Seven years ago, I found such a woman: she worked in publishing and she was bookish and funny. After months of patient bantering I convinced her to leave her fiancé, and our relationship immediately began to judder. Because we could crack each other up, I had not focused on her disclosure that she played the piano precisely but without passion, or her refusal to let me hear her play. I had not focused on her frequent recourse to litotes, in which affirmation is expressed by negating its opposite (but never really expressed): "Your article didn't feel like an eat-your-vegetables"; "I thought you weren't at all overclever." I had not focused on the way she met personal questions with all the easygoing candor of a Swiss bank. And I did not focus, for a long while, on her depression. But when someone is shaking with dry sobs at the far end of the couch, and the couch is a love seat, even a blockhead begins to wonder.

"I have some problems," she eventually admitted. She refused to specify further and glared at me with pure hatred for asking, if a look so shot through with beseeching can be called pure. I took her misery personally without feeling much personal responsibility—

her problems, not mine. That summer, I left town a lot, hoping that she'd get better while I was gone, as if misery were like pinkeye. Being helpful wasn't part of my plan, anyway: my plan was that she was going to save *me*.

I know, I know. But I was fairly depressed, myself, in those days. I was taking a lot of naps and tattooing my journal with laments. I was feeling lonely, of course; lonely and unappreciated (in hide-and-seek those who hide all too well always get mad at the seeker). At a house party that fall some friends and I played Smoke, the metaphor game. In terms of weather I was described as "overcast" and "a storm"; in terms of flavor, as "anise." Anise! I was trying to project a vintage Bordeaux and coming across as licorice.

I feared that the truth was even worse. I saw myself as a person lugging around a paint can full of walnut stain; if anyone got too close, the stain would slop all over them. So I tried to keep the brimming can to myself. But after she and I finally broke up, in mutual sadness and relief, I spent much of the next year stumbling around with the can in plain sight, splattering like Jackson Pollock as I tried to get her back. We reunited, sort of, a few times, and then she started seeing someone who lived far away. I chose that late date to finally promise complete transformation, into some-one who would intuit her deepest unspoken needs, who would give her acres of personal space, yet always be at hand to break her fall, a trusty fireman with his net. By then, she'd seen enough to know that we were fatally unsuited—that we were all too similar—and so she said, in Eeyore-like tones, "I don't feel the same way you do."

Like a total jackass, I replied, "I hereby withdraw my romantic remarks." When you're stricken, you can't think straight, and when you can't think straight, you can't banter. The word *hereby* can work in raillery, its lawyerliness carrying an ironic spin. But *here-by*—or *remarks*, for that matter—never works in actual conversa-tion. No true lover cries, "Pursuant to my suit I hereby append a compendium of not untender sentiments!" The tone was all wrong because I was no longer quite sure who I was supposed to be.

Other relationships followed, none particularly promising. One woman I was involved with for a few months told me, "Wit is your wooden leg." The reply "And your husband is yours" was on my lips, but I didn't say it. I didn't say it because I didn't really want her to leave him. Jab, jab, jab, stick and move.

Soon afterward, in the summer of 2000, I met Amanda. An accomplished food writer, she was pretty, smart, curious, affectionate, and stubborn. On our first date, I slipped into the old chaff-and-sparkle routine, but aside from asking a few deft questions, she was silent. When I walked her back to her apartment building and suggested another date, she gave me a dark-eyed look until I said, "Or, not . . .," and turned away.

She maintains, now, that she was nervous and thought she had said yes, but it was hardly a brilliant evening. You need two to banter. If the other person doesn't cooperate, you begin to sound, to your own ears, glib and anxious. You are not sparring, but shadowboxing. The analogy to masturbation becomes all too apparent.

The first night Amanda and I spent together, some weeks later, I turned to her before we went to sleep and said, "Hello, you." Not the most inspired utterance, perhaps, but not banter, either. Unfortunately, she misheard this as "I love you." And so she freaked out, quietly, suspecting that I was the sort of operator who said that to every woman he slept with. Partly as a result, she didn't say "I love you" to me for about six months. In the interim, she almost never called me by name, or even by a nickname. I wasn't "Tad," or "Mr. Tremendous," or even "the WASP Stallion." She kept her opinion of me in limbo, in the unvoiced gap between her recognition and her hopes: "Hey . . . want to get something to eat?" It reminded me of when I'd felt awkward around a girlfriend's parents, wondering how to address them if they never invited me to call them Bobo and Barky.

I knew that Amanda loved me but also that she doubted the wisdom of her attachment, as she'd rather quickly found the can of stain and stirred its inky depths. She took to patting my head a lot, prompting me to say, "Old Pokey, he was a good horse." I wasn't so good at being loved. Being loved requires you to stop cultivating every woman you meet; it requires you to pony up. Amanda didn't always say that much, but I knew she could banter at an emotional, rather than verbal, level—she could respond to my needs, mend her course, and zing back needs of her own. And so I reacted to my pleasure in seeing her, my delight in her brisk walk and cackling laugh, by staying away. A few months into our relationship, I landed in New York late at night after a reporting trip and went not to Amanda's but home to sleep. I called her from my apartment, saying I was just too tired and would see her tomorrow. She said, "Passionless fool!" and we both laughed. It was true. Not that I was passionless, but that I was a fool to hide it.

I had always been happiest expressing passion during the chase or retrospectively, after a relationship was over. (It was all a little sadistic.) Voicing passion in an ongoing relationship was much harder—it felt too naked. I slowly got better at telling Amanda my feelings, but it was months before I got around to mentioning, over pizza, that I'd been involved with a few of the women she'd met as my friends. Four of them, in fact. I'd kept this explosive detail to myself partly because she was more than a little jealous, and partly because I kept a lot of things to myself, out of long and mistrustful habit. It was only after I said it that I realized—duh!—that if I were her, I'd be furious and hurt.

She was furious and hurt. She said that I'd essentially hung her out to dry in every conversation she'd had with one of those friends. I tried to speed the conversation along ("What a relief to have *that* out of the way . . .") and then just buttoned up and took the heat.

Amanda eventually zeroed in on my mattress as the Indian burial ground of my rootless past. She announced that she could no longer sleep on it—too spooky. I had no great commitment to the mattress, but I felt strongly that being the banter king entailed keeping my own counsel, my own schedule, my own prerogatives, and, if it came to that, my own goddamn mattress. Cunning rejoinders came springing to mind: "Did *you* get a new mattress for our relationship?" and "Nobody sleeps on a *mattress*—shouldn't you be mad at my sheets?" and so on. And so on and on and on.

But all I said, when I finally opened my mouth, was "I told you about this because I love you." And then I went out and bought a new mattress.

How Not to Score

NICHOLAS WEINSTOCK

Even the most studious of men somehow flunk monogamy, our best intentions sullied by the inexplicable slipup or reckless lapse. And while there have been plenty of attempts to explain this phenomenon—from dissertations on *Homo sapiens* evolution to the unhelpful chestnut that *boys will be boys*—no theorist seems to have a solution for the propensity of men, with a little prompting, to cheat. Therefore, allow me to suggest one of my own. I propose that we committed men would be far better at avoiding affairs if we were to follow the same guidelines that, when we were single, helped us to have them.

I, for one, am happily married: boringly so, miraculously so, gratefully flabbergasted at having landed my wife. At precisely seven years of marriage, I find myself wholeheartedly itch-free. Nonetheless, I should confess that there have been affairs. Not affairs that I've *had*; not quite, not consummated; but they've been there, these things, rearing their pretty heads and lunging. This, to be honest, has come as a surprise. After all, I've never been much of a lady-killer. Gawky-limbed, funny-haired, and with a knack for sweet-talking girls into better relationships with their boyfriends, I was always a feeble bachelor. Now that I'm a feeble husband, that any woman has any extracurricular interest in me is startling. Nonetheless, I have been the clumsy recipient of female propositions. Moreover, I have found that dodging them takes practice. In fact, it takes training. Because while men around the world are experienced at the pursuit of lusty women, few of us know the subtler art of avoiding them.

Yet I have discovered that the tactics involved are one and the same. The very techniques that once improved my long-shot chances with sexy strangers can also, years later, be employed to escape them. Essentially, these strategies can be boiled down to three. These were the basic rules of the road when I was a hapless bachelor looking for flings. And since then, they have become the three golden rules that have helped me to keep myself, and my marriage, fling-free.

Rule Number One: *Location, Location, Location*

Back in my lame singlehood, whatever remote possibility I had of getting some action was as likely to hinge on my location as anything else. Good manners were helpful, good instincts were key, but more critical was the good fortune to be in the right place at the right time. In fact, that good fortune could, I gradually understood, be manufactured. This came as a revelation. We can create our own opportunities. We can—like chess players—actually pick up and move ourselves, relocate ourselves strategically in order to capture the queen.

I learned this golden rule just in time to practice it with Peggy Rogers. In sixth grade, I spent the long afternoon of February 14 lackadaisically pacing Peggy's street (a twenty-minute drive from, say, my street) with my obedient father parked in our family Wagoneer and incognito on a distant curb. Operation Valentine eventually worked: beginning that day, and with our "Hey-what-do-you–know?" conversation, I became, triumphantly, albeit temporarily, Peggy's boyfriend. And the lesson was clear. Simply by arranging a well-timed physical proximity to someone, you can set yourself up for physical proximity of a more meaningful sort.

Naturally, this discovery marked the start of a long era of hanging out by the girls' lockers in high school, joining female-dominated study groups in college and bumping semicoincidentally into love interests in their neighborhood bars. These are the covert operations that guys regularly undertake to sneak onto the radar, and perhaps into the hearts, of women. The trick, then, once I got married, was to make them into escape operations. Location and relocation remained as important as ever; yet instead of staging a well-timed appearance, the mission was to skillfully disappear.

That was my mission, for instance, with—well, let's call her Jen. Jen was older, and married, but discontentedly so; or at least that's the advertisement that beamed from her sea-green eyes when she stared (it actually seemed, inexperienced as I was, that she glared) at me for the first time. We had known each other when I was in college, if only peripherally; and now that we both found ourselves living in New York City and working in book publishing, we had arranged a vaguely editorial lunch. Then came the green glare. At the time I was dating the woman I'd eventually marry, who was away for the year in graduate school in Virginia. Upon learning this, Jen crooked an eyebrow and proposed drinks the next night. She plonked a hand on the back of my neck, pal-like, only she left it there. Then she squeezed. I begged off the drinks date and politely fled the restaurant. Only later did I realize I had proudly given her my card.

Her phone calls came casually at first. She seemed content to chat about nothing, with intentionally long pauses, once a week. Then every couple days. Soon she suggested we graduate to a dinner date. I fumbled through my packed imaginary schedule and reported that I was busy. Once she mentioned that she was going to be near my apartment over the weekend and could swing by. I mentioned my girlfriend, again, and claimed to be buried in manuscripts. It didn't help, one night, that we spotted each other at a Barnes and Noble book signing. When she turned from congratulating the author, cast me a beckoning look, and retreated into the Self-Improvement section, I saw my opportunity. I slipped down the escalator and out into the clean clarity of New York at night.

Eventually, heatedly, Jen called to say she had to see me. Her passion made no sense. I had given her so little to go on; I hadn't turned particularly handsome or fiscally successful in the years since we'd first met; nor had I been charming or scintillating enough during our brisk lunchtime reunion to have elicited anything like this festering lust. I would guess, looking back, that she had fallen for the idea of an affair: that a secret dalliance would provide her with a dose of escapism, a cinematic break from her marital reality; and that, lacking other candidates, she had hurriedly cast me as her male lead. In any case, she breathed through the phone that she and her husband were moving to Washington, D.C., in a few days. I congratulated her and had begun to enthuse about the greater Georgetown area ("Terrific place to raise kids") when she cut me off. We had one night left to see each other. I replied that unfortunately I had to work late. She said she would come by my office after hours, then, and hung up.

There was a time, of course, that this would have been welcome news. One night of romance with no ramifications. A sexually eager female hell-bent on bedding me and moving on. But I was too interested in my boundless future with Miss Virginia to louse it up for an hour atop a photocopy machine with Mrs. Robinson. Still, I figured I should stay at the office and meet Jen head-on. It would be downright rude to ditch her, volatile and needy as she clearly was. Besides, didn't I owe her a fuller explanation, perhaps a florid testimony of my love for another woman, a stirring treatise on fidelity thrown in for her sake? Sure, I'd be tempted, standing there in an empty office with the grabby woman a few inches away. Men, come to think of it, are always caught in such compromising positions, stammering to explain how they got there and how it wasn't their fault. But not me, I thought. Not tonight. I could resist.

Yet for the remainder of the afternoon, I found myself thinking back, strangely, and for the first time in more than a decade, to Peggy Rogers. Just as I once literally situated myself near a girl to get her attention, maybe I literally had to remove myself from this woman to free myself of hers. Lack of romance—just like romance—is a question of location. You can't cheat when you're not there. And sometimes that's the only way to be sure.

Leaving the office lobby, I cast a last wary look around and trudged home with the sense, for a few blocks, anyway, that I'd gone to an unnecessary extreme. I could have resisted her advances. We might have talked it through and parted as buddies. Instead I'd up and relocated, extricated myself preemptively, stranded the poor wacko with my vanishing act. But by the time I reached my apartment, any regret had turned to resolve. If location was everything, then the only one that interested me was Virginia.

Rule Number Two: *Add Ingredients Gradually*

If the real estate industry provides us with *location, location, location,* we can look to the culinary arts for rule number two. Single men—we eventually learn—are best off proceeding with patience, carefully nurturing our chances with women rather than barging in to give it a desperate shot. In other words, at the hopeful start of relationships, we ought to add our ingredients gradually. Dumping ourselves onto wary women is not only unsavory; as a method of cooking up romance, it stinks.

In college, I never had a chance with—hell, let's call her Skylar. She dated older men; she did fashionable drugs; she had a magazine-cover body (her torso alone was taller than me) and the glossy hauteur to match. Nonetheless, I gave it an occasional—and gradual—shot. I made a few attempts at offhanded humor in the Foreign Cultures class we shared, but never two days in a row. I coolly handed her my copy of the syllabus after she complained she'd lost hers; but when she griped that she'd lost her textbook, I pretended not to hear. Once I saw her in taut sweatpants and plugged into a Walkman on her way back from a run. I mouthed hello and kept mouthing soundlessly once she had halted and taken out her earphones, which for some reason she found hysterical. More important, I hustled off before she had put them back on. I was following the rule, not overextending, not making an ass of myself but rather making myself gently known. It was a kind of romantic water torture, this drip-drip creation of chemistry between us.

Naturally, with my luck, it was only once I was married that the chemistry experiment finally paid off.

Skylar was born to stride across crowded rooftop parties in downtown Manhattan, wearing something snug and belly-baring enough to attract the popping eyes and flashbulbs of a surrounding public. The only surprise, a few years ago, was that she was striding across that one toward me. We were reintroduced, unnecessarily, and were soon laughing about my college friends and her ex-boyfriends and wondering aloud, after several more paper-cupped vodkas, why we had never hooked up. She remembered me as funny. I could recite virtually every word I'd ever uttered near her. And now they had borne fruit, years later. A year and a half too late. I told her I was married. Her face didn't fall.

Instead, she left the party when I did and offered to buy me a quick beer next door. She was divorced, she confessed once we were seated on high barstools that accentuated the spectacle of her legs and left me dangling mine. Then she confessed she'd always been interested in me, but had assumed I was too intellectual for her. I cursed my A in Foreign Cultures and thought: This is the kind of thing that does it. This is why men have affairs. We see alluring potential; we can't help but gently and optimistically nurture it—and it is so hard not to reap that potential once it blooms before our eyes.

31

However, the key is not to forget the larger harvest. Much more important than my petty possible conquest was the lifelong partner who required that same steady investment herself. With any dalliance elsewhere, I would be failing to add to my marriage; in fact, I would be subtracting from it, whether I meant to or not. The daring spontaneity, the flirty humor and the jolts of charisma that I might devote to other women would be far better spent on the woman whose happiness would in turn brighten my life. The rule, now as ever, was to add ingredients gradually, and that meant building my marriage with the diligence of a master chef. Although I had skillfully heated things up with Skylar, I had to let them go. Such is the proud sadness of all great chefs who meticulously stir, infuse, and garnish only to give their best dishes away.

Rule Number Three: *Diversify Your Portfolio*

All my sexual life (I would call it my sexual "career" if that didn't suggest a reliable productivity), I seem to have striven for the new and different. Maybe we all do, in an ever-adolescent effort to broaden our horizons and add notches to our belts. In any case, my own scattershot passion has embraced all types. From homebodies to hardbodies, African-American to Icelandic, crew-cut to curly tresses and militant socialist to penitent Catholic, the women I have clumsily landed over the years make up a clashing mosaic of humanity, a kind of "We Are the World" chorus of disparate women charitably devoted—each for a fleeting, weak moment—to me. This is the way a lot of guys go forth in the single world: with an open-armed policy that not only allows for novelty but lustily embraces it. An unprecedented female characteristic or innovative amorous situation is generally cheered as a groundbreaking advance onto new terrain. We are encouraged, as if by a certified public accountant, to diversify our portfolio. And it's sound advice. After all, for a typical young man trying and failing to interest one kind of woman, it couldn't hurt to try another, and another after that.

The question, of course, with marriage, is how to continue to embrace life's voluptuous diversity without actually embracing anyone. Having been effectively trained to broaden our horizons, must we now shrink them tight as a ring?

My recent employment as a corporate speechwriter seemed a good job for a ring-wearer. Better money than book publishing; decent benefits and health care; only occasional travel away from home. It was rare, in fact, to have to embark on the sort of weekend trip to Las Vegas that I found myself taking two years ago to oversee a keynote speech at a trade show. Rarer still to be flirted with by the woman directly across the aisle. Half-Japanese, she was. Beautiful too. Tattoo on her hand.

Keiko—her real name was something close to that—began by commenting on my book. Literary, even. Large-chested. In Vegas for the weekend as well. She was attending the same convention, reporting on the thing for a national magazine. As a matter of fact, it turned out she was staying at my hotel. With her long sideways look, the cabin became pressurized. Like an automatic oxygen mask, out sprang my usual mention of my wife. And as usual, it didn't quite work. As we descended for our landing, Keiko wrote down my name and said we should get together to talk about books. I said something noncommittal and took comfort in the planetary size of the hotel.

Less comforting, however, was the sultry invitation that blinked on my hotel room voice mail the next night. And even less comforting was that Keiko was a kind of woman I'd never known. In my uncommitted past, such a novel flirtation would quickly have gotten the best of me. She was Japanese, for chrissake. A frigging hand tattoo. I was in *Vegas*. I had never been to Vegas, and I would probably never be again. This, staring me in the face, twisting my stomach, was a new life experience, an outward expansion. To forgo it would be to be limited forever to the familiar. To my East Coast primness, my clean-handed Western wife. To the disappointment of letting life's diverse options go by.

Which I did. I wrote my speech. I engaged in no further speech with Keiko. When I saw her from afar at the event—that convention hall was the size, and housed the population, of a capital city— I shrank into the shadows and out of the fluorescent fake daylight until she had turned gorgeously away. And although my thoughts over the weekend roamed from the possible placement of Keiko's other tattoos to a passing curiosity about her return-flight plans, they ultimately landed on my own plans to fly to Italy in a couple months for another speech. I decided to sneak my wife along for the trip. There was my diversity. We'd spend the weekend in northern Italy. There was the lush spontaneity of life. We would have secret meetings between speechwriting sessions. Sex in an unusual locale. Unexpected romantic options need not be forsaken nor should they. Enticing opportunities in all directions must be seized. It's just sleeping with optional, enticing women that is no longer—as they say in Vegas—in the cards. Everything else must be sampled. Even better, it can be shared.

I suppose I expected marriage to change all the rules. And I suppose it has; at the very least, it's reversed their purpose. Still I move my person to strategic locations when I don't necessarily trust my emotions to maneuver quite as nimbly. Still I'm careful to add steadily and subtly to a relationship, and I continue to diversify my romantic exploits whenever I can. The difference is that I no longer do so to get lucky; I *am* lucky, now, and determined to stay that way. This has meant making up golden rules and flailing to obey them. It's meant plodding effort and occasionally painful restraint and posing as a monk when, beneath my habit, I am as dirtily human as I've ever been. I guess the real difference between now and then is that I am blessed with another person who knows that: who's dirty herself; who poses, flirts, and retreats; and who would scoff at my stupid rules if I ever revealed them. Back when I strutted and fretted beneath the notice of girls, I longed to climb into their view. Now that I have fallen in love, I have no urge ever to climb out.

Companion Species

RICK MOODY

Among the aspects of my character that are owing to a youthful predilection for all things John Cheever is a boundless and irrational love of dogs, in particular a love for large, slobbering, affectionate dogs of the genus retriever. This love of retrievers runs across the color spectrum—yellow Labs and chocolate Labs being just as good as the more common and more absurdly affectionate black and golden varieties—and is so overpowering that I have often used it as a sort of character test for the near and dear. What kinds of dogs do you like? Anyone who has the gall to answer poodle, let's say, or basenji, or perhaps one of those varieties of dog that most closely resemble a slipper, is in my view extremely suspect.

I grew up around dogs. For example, we had a black Lab called Trouble. Trouble and I were all but exactly coeval, she being my elder by just a couple of months. She was a wonderful dog, great with kids, and absolutely appropriately named, in that she had a gustatory predilection for neighborhood garbage. Trouble was forever seeking little between-meal snacks from the garbage cans of our street, and she was inevitably coughing up the remnants of these snacks in the pantry or on the carpet in the den. Between vomiting episodes, she was as faithful as an animal could be. Her demise, by particularly grisly means—having eaten some bits of glass along with one of her feasts, she succumbed to internal bleeding—was hard for all of us.

Well, my parents were also divorcing at the time. This was hard too, although it is obviously a trauma that many people know well. In the aftermath of the divorce of my parents, I became a little skeptical about most things, about everything except dogs. And the New York Mets. And Pink Floyd. Chief among the institutions I thought suspect was marriage itself. Married people, I figured, were simpletons. Married people subsisted on a diet of lies, many of them told *by* themselves *to* themselves, many of these lies hurtful and many of them just plain delusional. People who talked up the prospect of getting married had no idea what they wanted, unless what they wanted was security in an insecure world. They wanted things they could not have in this mediated and disappointing place, certainty, stability, reliability, etc. I knew, or had a good idea that I knew, that fidelity was *the* big lie of marriage, that persons I had known in marriages, persons related to me in marriages, were out fucking around, drinking too much, jumping into bed, heedless of the costs to the foot soldiers of Generation X, and this made me bitter and also conferred on me the glory of inflexible certainty.

When the late seventies came with their punk rock revolution, I seemed to fall into a *movement,* if that's what it was, that had plenty of room for my kind of disgust. The domestic adventure, with its cars and houses and certificates of deposit, was laughable. So here's a big *fuck you,* I thought, to those people with their cautious and timid little lives, a big *fuck you* to them and their kids and their parents, a big *fuck you* to their conservative attitudes and their premature senescence. I had no intention of falling into this *lifestyle,* ever.

In truth, I was worse than I'm describing. Anyone in my college years who made the mistake of being in a relationship with me (I'm kindly omitting their names) and who dared to imply, no matter how faintly, that I might owe them something, that I might be obligated to them in a certain way, by virtue of my transient intimations of devotion, these persons ended up with a mouthful of ashes for their trouble. Sometimes on the spot, sometimes after a few weeks.

It wasn't that I wanted to be an asshole. As I have described elsewhere at length, I was also having a little bit of trouble with drinking and other things, so it wasn't as if I were fully operational on matters of the heart. In fact, there was little I *was* interested in back then, except perhaps Samuel Beckett, Virginia Woolf, or Elvis Costello. But I suppose, in my way, I wanted what everyone else wants, to have purpose and to feel *love,* whatever that was. When I was being honest, I saw happy, loving couples traversing the quadrangles and I wondered what they knew that I didn't.

In short, a retriever knows more than I knew about love, fidelity, and commitment. And the person who was suffering most for all my arguments was me. I was the person who had refused to kiss my mother for ten years, not even a peck on the cheek, I was the person who had never told my high school girlfriend of two years that I loved her, I was the person who would have a good laugh anytime the idea of a lifelong commitment came up. And I was the one crashing every party I could find on Saturday nights, drunker and drunker, hoping that somebody would just hold me, or consent to be held, even as I sneered at the pool of available hostages. Nobody cared about my Stalinist program of love, they just avoided talking about it with me.

A period of genuine mental illness followed not long after, and then I woke up in the late eighties not having had a proper relationship, date, one-night stand, or anything, in a year and a half. I decided that I needed in some fashion to address the fact that I was unsuccessful in human relationships, of any kind, that I was not good at loving other people, had felt no love, had known no love, was in danger of never having the thing that made life tolerable for so many others, and while this might make for experimental fiction, it didn't make for a pleasant life. I was in my early thirties.

Have I mentioned that I always hated cats? I always hated cats. We had a Maine coon cat when I was ten, a beautiful big black thing with an enormous tail. It died precipitously, of some kidney ailment. It peed blood all over the sofa that my mother bought for us when we had little other furniture. The garish demise of the coon cat was a christening for the notion of the broken home. Not long after, there was a stray called Gypsy. She got knocked up several times the first year we had her, and the kittens in her second litter died one by one in the front-hall closet. I don't know why Gypsy hadn't been spayed, on the occasion of her tenancy in our house. We just didn't immediately get around to things like this. Once she was fixed, however, she became a proper house cat, and she endured for another six or eight years. Not that I paid any attention to her. I didn't live at home after I was thirteen, since I was away at school. When I *was* home, Gypsy came to sit on my lap, once or twice a year, and I pushed her off, because it cramped my style. The whole idea of sitting in one position just so that a feline could have a warm spot on which to perch, this is the kind of idea that gains no traction with a teenager.

According to tradition, therefore, I avoided the kinds of people who were too attached to their cats. Women who talked too much about cats were suspect. (They were undoubtedly going to start collecting dozens of strays, and I didn't want anything to do with this.) People with two or more cats, in particular, were to be shunned. Of course, there was additionally the problem of where to put the cat box in small NYC apartments. I hated having to trip over the cat box on the way to the bathroom, and I hated having to listen to the cat hack up its hair balls, and I hated the near constant vomiting episodes of the cats I knew. These women with their two or more cats, they just didn't have time for human beings.

In 1994, after praying, actually praying, to meet someone with whom I might be able to have a genuine relationship, I made the acquaintance of a woman in Chicago. Because it all happened *fast,* I decided that I would overlook a certain fact that would normally have ruled out this particular relationship, viz, that she shared her apartment with two cats. It was probably that she lived in Chicago that made this tolerable. I only had to visit with the cats occasionally.

The long-distance feature of our romance lasted for a year or more, and since I was not particularly enamored with *commitment,* it was pretty comfortable. I went to Chicago, a city I grew to adore, once or twice a month, and when I was feeling lonely in New York, Amy would turn up and pry me loose from my solitude. In this way, I began to see that the time I spent alone, usually strung-together days of compulsive activities like work, computer games, Web surfing, and masturbation, was actually substandard time. I was *against* myself, when alone, despite that I had always felt really *free,* and what can be wrong with feeling really *free?*

My *commitment tolerance level,* if one were to graph it rudely onto a thermometer, as in one of those United Way signs, was on the rise. I was by no means out of the woods, and I did pull the occasional bachelor-like stunt. In fact, I'd argue that I will never entirely get out of the woods, since the dark, murderous aspect of masculinity, the part that is about fighting off the other suitors and eating their still-beating hearts, the part that is always looking over a shoulder for the next competitor, that part is in me yet and always will be. Still, I began to feel a difference. It certainly was not that I had met *the one true love,* etc., which is a kind of thinking that I find naïve, or even moronic. But there was a difference.

One event that certainly brought about change, an event about which I have also written before, was my sister's death in November of 1995. A disagreeable feature of the sudden death in the family is that you find yourself taking a tally of your friends and family. You look around, you think, Did this guy show up? Does this woman care about what I'm going through? It's a variety of selfishness, and I was in no way proud of it, but I found myself doing this nonetheless, to a subliminal purpose: the circling of the wagons. The people I really loved were in the circle, they *were* the inner circle, and the people who didn't somehow measure up stayed on the outside. Suddenly the relationships that I'd disparaged in my twenties were the only relationships I had, whatever their tenor, and these people, of course, could die any day. Therefore, I didn't have the time to fuck around with grudge-holding. Which doesn't mean that the near and dear were faultless. But if they were going to die, I wanted to know that the channels were open and the cards on the table. My sister died without warning, and I didn't get to tell her good-bye or that I loved her, and I hope I never have to go through something like that again.

The other thing that happened was that Amy from Chicago, who, in romantic terms, could have gone either way on me, moved to New York to be available during the hard times described above. This was an incredible kindness, and one I scarcely deserved. But I grew into it. Within a couple of years, I got rid of my apartment in Brooklyn, bought a house up the coast, and we started dividing our time, back and forth, between our two addresses, sort of living together, something I had promised I would never do again after the experiment in 1992 with the woman who hectored me because, she claimed, I didn't change the toilet paper often enough.

Naturally, when Amy moved to New York, she brought along the two cats.

One cat was called simply Cat. He had the dignity that you'd associate with such a simple name. He was gigantic, black, and slow-moving, but completely domesticated. He liked to be held, and he even groomed Amy occasionally, while she slept, so that she'd wake and find his sandpapery tongue all over her. I started to like him mainly because he was implacable. He liked to be released into the hall of the apartment building, where he would, given the opportunity, gallop to the farthest end, like a freed slave, to smell the doors of other residents. Amy took him up to her roof too,

41

which has a panoramic view of lower Manhattan. She would hold him in her arms and walk along the perimeter showing him the sights. This was the best of all worlds for Cat, there was nothing better, except perhaps for chasing Moo, the other cat, of whom more in a moment. Cat was slower and less agile, but quite a bit more violent, despite having no front claws.

However, by the time I was on the scene, Cat was already declining. It started in little ways. One morning we woke to what seemed like Cat having some kind of seizure, complete with strange dancing movements. The vet turned up nothing. Then there was the growing incontinence. It wasn't that he occasionally missed the cat box, it was that he wasn't even in the right room, and as with many cats, knowing he had failed in this responsibility would send him into paroxysms of remorse. He'd start running around the house howling uncharacteristically. When it got to be everyday, cleaning up Cat's wastes on the bedding, on the carpets, and so forth, Cat's fate was sealed. Of course, he was also partially blind and all but deaf. (The blind eyes of a cat are an amazing thing to behold. One of Cat's eyes became completely opaque, really more like a marble than an eye.) There was the dandruff too, and the refusal to eat. I think Cat was in his middle teens, and he had made many journeys, from Ohio to Chicago and back to Ohio and then to New York City, but now there would be no more journeys.

Amy managed, through a friend, to find a veterinarian who would euthanize in situ. Cat had a mortal terror of veterinarians, and so this was a good strategy since it allowed Cat to go out with a little bit of his dignity intact. I remember thinking that it was sad but that's how it was with *companion species,* they ate glass and pissed blood all over the new couch. They came and they went, and they were not people, but you did your best.

The veterinarian was a mortician, really, since he had this specialized practice, and he was accustomed, no doubt, to completely distraught pet owners. But we were *not* completely distraught, were we? He examined Cat and got a history and told us we were doing the right thing, but how so? How is taking a life a good thing? Maybe, when it alleviates suffering. Amy told the vet that we were going up to the roof, because that was Cat's favorite place, and it was a beautiful day, warm and sunny, with bright skies. The first shot was to sedate the animal, after which we would wait a couple of minutes. The second shot would stop his heartbeat.

Amy gave Cat a good walk around on the roof, and he was certainly in his element, the master of his fortune, and then we sat with him on some of the porch furniture up there and the vet gave him shot number one, and when the needle went in, Cat gave a long, low, outraged howl, and I remember thinking that this was going to be the last sound Cat made and found myself, much against my character and my instincts, sobbing, in a way that I had not sobbed since my sister had died. I actually had to excuse myself, for a moment, from the process of Cat's eyelids getting heavy, and his wobbling around trying to organize himself into a circle to go to sleep. I was leaning against the roof railing sobbing uncontrollably, because I had learned something you only need to learn once, that grief calls unto grief. There's a reservoir, and it's a reservoir that never seems to get emptied.

When I got back, Cat's eyes were closed, and he was coiled in that sweet, vulnerable coil of the sleeping feline, and then Cat was given the second shot, and Amy, who had managed to hold him before he was asleep, told him that he had always been a good cat, and she thanked him, and then he was zipped up into a bag and he was gone. It was almost too neat.

We went downstairs back to Amy's apartment, and on the way we made jokes about how Moo was always the less interesting of the two of the cats, and how fitting, in a way, that the less beguiling cat hangs around longest. Moo was shy and would hide in closets and under beds for days. She vocalized too much, so that if even the least thing was out of whack, a suitcase in the middle of the floor,

43

she would run around wailing about it, before hiding behind the garbage can. She had to be fed at the exact same time every day, and she had to be fed the exact same thing, and you had better go to bed at the exact same time every night, or she would actually try to herd you to bed. Also, she was kind of unattractive. She'd been a runt once, with gigantically oversize ears, but now she was a runt that had gotten fat. Bunched onto her runty frame was this big, pear-shaped cat ass. She was like someone's maiden aunt, always showing up for holiday dinners with Rice Krispies squares.

Well, I fell for her too. I fell for the maiden aunt. I didn't even like cats, but the maiden aunt figured out that I liked to watch television on the floor, and when her elderly fear-of-death need for constant stroking and attention seemed to set in, not long after the passing of Cat, suddenly I was bonding with Moo, the fat runt, and I didn't even like her all that much. I didn't even like cats! And I sure didn't like being in a house watching television and ordering in Thai food and talking about what seeds we were going to order for the garden that summer. Taken as an aggregate, I found the relationship business hard to fathom, but here I was doing it, even respecting it.

Somewhere in here Amy asked me to marry her. I know it usually goes the other way, but it should be obvious by now that I would find ways never to ask this particular question, and *never* was not a timetable that was acceptable to Amy. We had been together five or six years. She wanted what she wanted, for which I cannot blame her. I thought, I'm just not the sort of person who does this sort of thing. I'm the sort of person who has been broken on the rack of matrimony! My baby food was matrimonial failure! Why ask me? Go ask one of those happy-looking guys with the pleated pants! One of those guys who sells things!

But I admired Amy for knowing what she wanted, because I had no idea what I wanted, beyond wanting to keep writing and listening to a lot of CDs and maybe having the occasional piece of pie. I tabled the whole thing for a couple more years.

When it came up next, I was near to turning forty. Amazing what a numerical transition can do to a person's thinking. Suddenly the imminence of death! Suddenly the possibility of decrepitude! And baldness! And diminishing levels of testosterone, to the tune of one percent per annum! And now we were close to celebrating a decade together. My late sister's kids, the kids she'd left behind, were in their teens, and a real bond with them had become part of our lives. It was an attachment that I'd never really imagined I was going to have with kids. I'd watched them grow up and I really loved watching them growing up, and I loved belittling Adam Sandler in their company. I loved complaining about their music and giving them books to read. And I loved listening to them. And so I started to feel that I already had a family, whether I was ready for one or not. And I already had a wife whether I wanted one or not. And I had already embarked on the part of being committed that I had never thought I was able to do, for being too neurotic and too vulnerable and having too strange a job. I was already showing up most days, and I was already thinking every morning that I was going to do my best to bring something into the life of this other person instead of always thinking or hoping that this other person would be the one doing stuff *for me*. I had started showing up in material ways, making a difference, offering support and counsel, and it made me feel a little better about life and myself. Not much, but a little.

In short, though a circuitous route, I had become responsible. I didn't know how it had happened, and I'm a little embarrassed by it, and I'm certainly embarrassed by talking about it, but it happened, and there was really no reason now, besides sheer obstinacy, not to *formalize the commitment,* which was how I put it when I asked Amy's father if it would be okay with him. There was a stunned silence while her father and mother tried to figure out what I was talking about.

There were a lot of hoops to jump through later, but that's for another time. My hypothesis today is that commitment isn't in strategizing about a trip to the altar, it's about how something as seemingly unimportant as learning to like cats led to my sense that I was already committed to my wife, and that commitment was a thing not to be avoided, but a thing to take pride in, and a thing to improve at, and a thing to watch change and grow. That's what happened. While I was avoiding getting married, I was starting to like cats, starting to accept that cats would do what they needed to do, and by the time I was certain that I liked cats, it was just a short hop to the altar, and all of that madness.

Right now, we're thinking about getting a kitten.

Old Faithful

DAVID SEDARIS

Out of nowhere I developed this lump. I think it was a cyst or a boil, one of those words you associate with trolls, and it was right on my tailbone, like a peach pit wedged into the top of my crack. That's what it felt like anyway. I was afraid to look. At first it was just this insignificant knot, but as it grew larger, it started to hurt. Sitting became difficult, and forget about lying on my back or bending over. By day five my tailbone was throbbing and I told myself, just as I had the day before, that if this kept up, I was going to see a doctor. "I mean it," I said. I even went so far as to pull out the phone book and turn my back on it, hoping that the boil would know that I meant business and go away on its own. But of course it didn't.

All of this took place in London, which is cruelly, insanely expensive. My boyfriend, Hugh, and I went to the movies one night, and our tickets cost a total of forty dollars, this after spending sixty on pizzas. And these were minipizzas, not much bigger than pancakes. Given the price of a simple evening out, I figured that a doctor's visit would cost around the same as a customized van. More than the money, though, I was afraid of the prognosis. "Lower-back cancer," the doctor would say. "It looks like we'll have to remove your entire bottom."

Actually, this being England, he'd probably have said *bum*, a word I have never really cottoned to. The sad thing is that they could remove my ass and most people wouldn't even notice. It's so insubstantial that the boil was actually an improvement, something like a bustle but fleshy and filled with poison. The only real drawback was the pain.

For the first few days I kept my discomfort to myself, thinking all the while of what a good example I was setting. When Hugh feels bad, you hear about it immediately. A tiny splinter works itself into his palm and he claims to know exactly how Jesus must have felt on the cross. He demands sympathy for insect bites and paper cuts, while I have to lose at least a quart of blood before I get so much as a pat on the hand.

One time in France we were lucky enough to catch an identical stomach virus. It was a twenty-four-hour bug, the kind that completely empties you out and takes away your will to live. You'd get a glass of water, but that would involve standing, and so instead you just sort of stare toward the kitchen, hoping that maybe one of the pipes will burst, and the water will come to you. We both had the exact same symptoms, yet he insisted that his virus was much more powerful than mine. I suspected the same thing, so there we were, competing over who was the sickest.

"You can at least move your hands," he said.

"No," I told him, "it was the *wind* that moved them. I have no muscle control whatsoever."

"Liar."

"Well, that's a nice thing to say to someone who'll probably die during the night. Thanks a lot, pal, I appreciate it."

At such times you have to wonder how things got to this point. You meet someone and fall in love, then thirteen years later you're lying on the floor in a foreign country, promising, hoping, as a matter of principle, that you'll be dead by sunrise. "I'll show you," I moaned, and then I must have fallen back to sleep.

When Hugh and I bicker over who is in the most pain, I think back to my first boyfriend, who I met while in my late twenties. Something about our combination was rotten, and as a result we competed over everything, no matter how petty. When someone laughed at one of his jokes, I would need to make that person laugh harder. If I found something at a yard sale, he would have to find something better—and so on. My boyfriend's mother was a handful, and every year, just before Christmas, she would go in for a mammogram, knowing she would not get the results until after the holidays. The remote possibility of cancer was something to hang over her children's heads, just out of reach, like mistletoe, and she took great pleasure in arranging it. The family would gather and she'd tear up, saying, "I don't want to spoil your happiness, but this may well be our last Christmas together." Other times, if somebody had something going on—a wedding, a graduation—she'd go in for exploratory surgery, anything to capture and hold attention. By the time I finally met her, she did not have a single organ that had not been touched by human hands. "Oh, my God," I thought, watching her cry on our living room sofa, "my boyfriend's family is more fucked-up than my own." I mean, this actually bothered me.

We were together for six years, and when we finally broke up, I felt like a failure, a divorced person. I now had what the self-help books called relationship baggage, which I would carry around for the rest of my life. The trick was to meet someone with similar baggage, and form a matching set, but how would one go about finding such a person? Bars were out, I knew that much. I met my first boyfriend at a place called The Man Hole—not the sort of name that suggests fidelity. It was like meeting someone at Fisticuffs and then complaining when he turned out to be violent. To be fair, he had never actually promised to be monogamous. That was my idea, and though I tried my hardest to convert him, the allure of other people was just too great.

Most all of the gay couples I knew at that time had some sort of an arrangement. Boyfriend A could sleep with someone else as long as he didn't bring him home, or as long as he *did* bring him home, and boyfriend B was free to do the same. It was a good setup for those who enjoyed variety and the thrill of the hunt, but to me it was just scary, and way too much work—like having one job while applying for another. One boyfriend was all I could handle, all I *wanted* to handle, really, and while I found this to be perfectly natural, my friends saw it as a form of repression and came to view me as something of a puritan. "Am I?" I wondered. But there were buckles to polish, and stones to kneel upon, and so I put the question out of my mind.

I needed a boyfriend as conventional as I was, and luckily I found one—just met him one evening through a mutual friend. I was thirty-three at the time, and Hugh had just turned thirty. Like me, he had recently broken up with someone, and had moved to New York to start over. His former boyfriend had been a lot like mine, and we spent our first few weeks comparing notes. "Did he ever say he was going out for a sub and then—"

"—hook up with someone he'd met that afternoon on a bus? Yes!"

We had a few practical things in common as well, but what really brought Hugh and me together was our mutual fear of abandonment and group sex. It was a foundation, and we built on it, adding our fears of AIDS and pierced nipples, of commitment ceremonies and the loss of self-control. In dreams sometimes I'll come across a handsome stranger waiting in my hotel room. He's usually someone I've seen earlier that day, on the street or in a television commercial, and now he's naked and beckoning me toward the bed. I look at my key, convinced that I have the wrong room, and when he springs forward and reaches for my zipper, I run for the door, which is inevitably made of snakes or hot tar, one of those maddening, hard-to-clean building materials so often used in dreams. The handle moves this way and that, and while struggling to grab it, I stammer an explanation as to why I can't go through with this. "I have a boyfriend, see, and, well, the thing is that he'd kill me if he ever found out I'd been, you know, unfaithful or anything."

Really, though, it's not the fear of Hugh's punishment that stops me. I remember once riding in the car with my dad. I was twelve, and it was just the two of us, coming home from the bank. We'd been silent for blocks, when out of nowhere he turned to me saying, "I want you to know that I've never once cheated on your mother."

"Ummm. Okay," I said. And then he turned on the radio and listened to a football game.

Years later I mentioned this incident to a friend, who speculated that my father had said this specifically because he *had* been unfaithful. "That was a guilty conscience talking," she said, but I knew that she was wrong. More likely my father was having some problem at work and needed to remind himself that he was not completely worthless. It sounds like something you'd read off a movie poster, but sometimes the sins you haven't committed are all you have to hold on to. If you're really desperate, you might need to grope, saying, for example, "I've never killed anyone with a hammer" or "I've never stolen from anyone who didn't deserve it." But whatever his faults, my dad did not have to stoop quite that low.

I have never cheated on a boyfriend, and as with my father, it's become part of my idea of myself. In my foiled wet dreams I can glimpse at what my life would be like without my perfect record, of how lost I'd feel without this scrap of integrity, and the fear is enough to wake me up. Once awake though, I tend to lie there, wondering if I've made a grave mistake.

In books and movies infidelity always looks so compelling, so *right*. Here are people who defy petty conventions and are rewarded with only the tastiest bits of human experience. Never do they grow old or suffer the crippling panic I feel whenever Hugh gets spontaneous and suggests we go to a restaurant.

"A restaurant? But what will we talk about?"

"I don't know," he'll say. "What does it matter?"

Alone together I enjoy our companionable silence, but it creeps me out to sit in public, propped in our chairs like a couple of mummies. At a nearby table there's always a couple in their late seventies, blinking at their menus from behind thick glasses.

"Soup's a good thing," the wife will say, and the man will nod or grunt or fool with the stem of his wineglass. Eventually he'll look my way, and I'll catch in his eyes a look of grim recognition. "We are your future," he seems to say. "Get used to it."

I'm so afraid that Hugh and I won't have anything to talk about that now, before leaving home, I'll comb the papers and jot down a half dozen topics that might keep a conversation going at least through the entrées. The last time we ate out, I prepared by reading both the *Herald Tribune* and *The Animal Finder's Guide,* a quarterly publication devoted to exotic pets and the nuts who keep them. The waiter took our orders, and as he walked away, I turned to Hugh saying, "So, anyway, I hear that monkeys can really become surly once they reach breeding age."

"Well, I could have told you *that,*" he said. "It happened with my own monkey."

I tried to draw him out, but it saddens Hugh to discuss his childhood monkey. "Oh, Maxwell," he'll sigh, and within a minute he'll have started crying. Next on my list were the five warning signs of depression amongst captive camels, but I couldn't read my handwriting, and the topic crashed and burned after sign number two: an unwillingness to cush. At a nearby table an elderly woman arranged and rearranged the napkin in her lap. Her husband stared at a potted plant and I resorted to the

Tribune. "Did, you hear about those three Indian women who were burned as witches?"

"What?"

"Neighbors accused them of casting spells and burned them alive."

"Well, that's horrible," he said, slightly accusatory, as if I myself had had a hand in it. "You can't go around burning people alive, not in this day and age."

"I know it, but—"

"It's sick is what it is. I remember once when I was living in Somalia there was this woman . . ."

"Yes!" I whispered, and then I looked over at the elderly couple, thinking, *See, we're talking about witch burnings!* It's work, though, and it's always *my* work. If left up to Hugh, we'd just sit there acting like what we are, two people so familiar with one another they could scream. Sometimes, when finding it hard to sleep, I'll think of when we first met, of the newness of each other's body, and my impatience to know everything about this person. Looking back, I should have taken it more slowly, measured him out over the course of fifty years rather than cramming him in so quickly. By the end of our first month together, he'd been so thoroughly interrogated that all I had left was breaking news— what little had happened in the few hours since I'd last seen him. Were he a cop or an emergency-room doctor, there might have been a lot to catch up on, but like me, Hugh works alone, so there was never much to report. "I ate some potato chips," he might say, to which I'd reply, "What kind?" or "That's funny, so did I!" More often than not we'd just breathe into our separate receivers.

"Are you still there?"

"I'm here."

"Good. Don't hang up."

"I won't."

*   *   *

In New York we slept on a futon. I took the left side and would lie awake at night, looking at the closet door. In Paris we got a regular bed in a room just big enough to contain it. Hugh would fall asleep immediately, the way he's always done, and I'd stare at the blank wall, wondering about all the people who'd slept in this room before us. The building dated from the seventeenth century, and I envisioned musketeers in tall, soft boots, pleasuring the sorts of women who wouldn't complain when sword tips tore the sheets. I saw gentlemen in top hats and sleeping caps, women in bonnets and berets and beaded headbands, a swarm of phantom copulators all looking down and comparing my life to theirs.

After Paris came London, and a bedroom on the sixth floor with windows looking onto neat rows of Edwardian chimney tops. A friend characterized it as "a Peter Pan view," and now I can't see it any other way. I lie awake thinking of someone with a hook for a hand, and then, inevitably, of youth, and whether I have wasted it. Twenty-five years ago I was twenty-two, a young man with his whole sexual life ahead of him. How had 9,125 relatively uneventful days passed so quickly, and how can I keep it from happening again? In another twenty-five years I'll be seventy-two, and twenty-five years after that I'll be one of the figures haunting my Paris bedroom. Is it morally permissible, I wonder, to cheat *after* death? Is it even called cheating at that point? What are the rules? Do I have to wait a certain amount of time, or can I just jump or, as the case may be, seep right in?

During the period that I had my boil, these questions seemed particularly relevant. The pain was always greater after dark, and by the sixth night I was fairly certain that I was dying. Hugh had gone to sleep hours earlier, and it startled me to hear his voice. "What do you say we lance that thing?" he said.

It's the sort of question that takes you off guard. "Did you just use the verb *to lance*?" I asked.

He turned on the lights.

"Since when did you learn to lance boils?"

"I didn't," he said. "But I bet I could teach myself."

With anyone else I'd put up a fight, but Hugh can do just about anything he sets his mind to. This is a person who welded the plumbing pipes at his house in Normandy, then went into the cellar to make his own cheese. There's no one I trust more than him, and so I limped to the bathroom, that theater of home surgery, where I lowered my pajama bottoms and braced myself against the towel rack, waiting as he sterilized the needle.

"This is hurting me a lot more than it's hurting you," he said. It was his standard line, but I knew that this time he was right. Worse than the boil was the stuff that came out of it, a horrible custard streaked with blood. What got to me, and got to him even worse, was the stench, which was unbearable, and unlike anything I had come across before. It was, I thought, what evil must smell like, not an evil *person*, but the wicked ideas that have made him that way. How could a person continue to live with something so rotten inside him? And so much of it! The first tablespoon gushed out on its own power, like something from a geyser. Then Hugh used his fingers and squeezed out the rest. "How are you doing back there?" I asked, but he was dry-heaving and couldn't answer.

When my boil was empty, he doused it with alcohol and put a bandage on it, as if it had been a minor injury, a shaving cut, a skinned knee, something normal he hadn't milked like a dead cow. And this, to me, was worth at least a hundred of the hundred and one nights of Sodom. Back in bed I referred to him as Sir Lance-A-Lot.

"Once is not a lot," he said.

This was true, but Sir Lance Occasionally lacks a certain ring. "Besides," I said, "I know you'll do it again if I need you to. We're an elderly monogamous couple, and this is all part of the bargain."

The thought of this kept Hugh awake that night, and still does. We go to bed and he stares toward the window as I sleep soundly beside him, my bandaged boil silently weeping onto the sheets.

Love to Hate Me

DAVID GRAND

1. Laura (1988–90)

She had a narrow face and aquiline nose, a forehead like that of an Eastern Orthodox icon. Fixed just above the left corner of her upper lip was a mole the size of a small dollop of chocolate. If she'd had a different physiognomy—if she were, say, short and plump, if her face were more round—her features could easily have befitted an attractive peasant girl, but, elongated as she was, tall and thin and elegant as she was, Laura was an idiosyncratic beauty who, at nineteen, had yet to realize that she was stunning. Her perception of herself was arrested somewhere in her awkward, gangly years— when her nose was outgrowing the rest of her body, when she was all akimbo at the elbows and knees.

We lived in the same boardinghouse during the summer of 1988. She had come to Berkeley to see friends. I was taking classes at the university. We used to cross paths in the dusty chaparral trails in the hills above Piedmont, and when we found that we had this escape in common, we started spending time up there together, hiking and running and talking. I imagine what initially attracted me to her was that unlike the more classically beautiful women that she surrounded herself with, Laura led with her intellect and sharp wit. When she found it to her advantage, she wasn't shy to express cruel dismissals of people she found irritating. She was a natural satirist and clever gossip and had a solar flare for ridicule. When I first found myself in her presence, I was overcome by a giddy sensation of Icarus-like carelessness, as if I were risking incineration.

I liked women who made me feel this way. I liked intelligent and ambitious and critical women who had the potential to do damage. Rarely did I fall for a woman who didn't have ambiguous feelings about me, at best. I'm not sure I fully understand the psychology behind this, but I suspect it was largely born out of my parents' divorce and its messy fallout.

In 1977, when I was eight years old, my mother, a schoolteacher from Middle Village, Queens, served divorce papers on my father, a plumber from Bensonhurst, Brooklyn. The separation was difficult. The divorce was bitter. The aftermath, all-out guerrilla war. Within a year, my father—whom I had loved and admired, with whom I had allied myself during the breakup—had taken on the tactics of a wronged Kleistian figure. And we—my mother, my little brother, and I—had become the enemy he was determined to annihilate. He deliberately drove his business into bankruptcy so as not to have to pay child support. And then he concocted elaborate lies about my mother, whom he made out to be a whore and a drug addict and a woman so self-centered she couldn't possibly love me and my brother. His plan was to brainwash us, to have us naïvely collude in a conspiracy to prove to a judge that she was an unfit mother.

With my father's lies firmly voiced in my head, I grew to loathe my mother, and as time passed, I felt more and more anxious to escape from her. So anxious that one night in the upstairs hallway of our house, I tackled her to the floor, pinned her down, and spat curses at her face. When I let her up, my petite mother, after realizing that I could physically dominate her, was so scared of me that she ordered me out of the house and onto the street. She packed a Hefty bag full of my clothes and drove me to my father's apartment. When my father opened the door to his naked studio with its rollaway bed and one cracked dish and one bent fork, I remember his face looking not worried or concerned, but, rather, sinisterly proud, as if he had accomplished exactly what he'd set out to do. He'd dealt the devastating blow.

Apparently the death blow to my mother's pride mattered more to him than I did. The following morning he put me and my green trash bag of belongings into his car. He drove me to school, and at the school's entrance, in front of all the other kids, he unloaded me and my bag and drove off. I skipped all my classes that day and wandered the streets until late in the evening, at which point I returned to my mother, who, reluctantly, opened the door just wide enough to let me in.

Some months later, my mother sold the house and all of our furniture and toys, and we fled New York for L.A. There I would be raised by my mother and the wayward women she seemed to collect annually, women who were recently divorced, or who were coming out of bad live-in relationships. She invited them into our small apartment on the Westside, where they took up residence on our couch for months at a time, and during their stays I listened to and strongly identified with their various complaints and observations about the shortcomings of men. On the one hand, by participating in these conversations, I was thoroughly reprogrammed, fixed of the damage done by my father—I became sensitive to what women wanted from a man, to how a man should behave, and was no longer a misogynist-in-the-making. On the other hand, I developed an acute fear that, as a man, I would never be able to give enough of myself to a woman to satisfy her. Compounding my fear that all men were dogs was the legacy of my father, whom I no longer knew (I've remained estranged from him to this day), but whom I was convinced I had the potential to become. My father was the maddest of mongrel dogs, ergo, I too would one day start foaming at the mouth.

This was a foregone conclusion, and so like some kind of Holy

Roller I was always on the lookout for the devil inside me, for the brutish flaws that would be released by some genetic time capsule. To ward off the evil within, I devised my own form of exorcism: I practiced the bilious art of self-hatred and performed toxic rituals of self-destruction. Thus, to love me was to love, in part, watching me hate myself.

Laura became spectator to my self-laceration during our summer in Berkeley. She appreciated my self-deprecation, my morose fatalism, my obsession with death and occasional difficulty masking sadness. She liked the dark humor and all the anxious-soul searching and the quiet intensity with which I paid attention to her. I was a morbid fascination. Something alien, to hold at arm's length.

She was equally curious to me and made me feel equally on edge—for I knew no one like Laura. Descended from a Boston Brahmin family, she had attended a Massachusetts boarding school and as a student at Barnard had spent a year abroad in London. Her father was a composer and a professor at Smith, whose work had been performed at Lincoln Center. Her mother was a housewife who tended to her gardens at houses in Northampton and on the Cape. Pedigree and privilege aside, what I found most unusual and disarming was the genuine affection Laura felt for her parents and her sisters, that she felt a physical longing for the places where she had grown up. It all sounded so solid and comfortable, and so unlike my own world of worries.

The sharpness that I observed in Laura's character when she was with her girlfriends dulled considerably in my company, especially when we were alone in my room. We spent many nights there quietly talking into the early mornings, and at such hours she had an incredible capacity to listen and sort me out, making me feel as if my life wasn't as trivial and meaningless as I feared it to be. She stood up to my morose fatalism and turned it on its head, to the point that I felt obligated to better myself. When I was with her, I never wanted to be anywhere else, and the more time I spent with

60

her, the more I wanted to see her. But true to her good judge of character, she kept an emotional distance. We were friends, she would say as she lay half-naked in my bed while I massaged her back, we were good friends. And because she kept her distance so well, it was impossible to know exactly how she felt about me. And because of this, all of a sudden, like pathetic little Pip in *Great Expectations* hoping to win the heart of Estella, I wanted to win Laura's approval.

When we parted at the end of the summer, it didn't take much for me to realize that I was in love with her. When I returned to L.A. and she to New York, in keeping with the quiet tone of our late-night chats, we started writing long, intimate letters to each other, letters that constantly preoccupied me and made me feel so restless that I couldn't sleep. To wear down my insomnia, I would drive to the Santa Monica bluffs and write to her from a bench overlooking the ocean. When I could afford it, I booked airline tickets to New York and wandered around the city waiting to spend a night or two with her. And when I heard that she would be spending her junior year in France, I planned a trip around the world that would end in Paris. I thought that if I arrived there at the beginning of the spring with a letter written to her from all the places I wanted to see because of her, such a gesture might help her reconsider our relationship and move her closer to me.

In Hong Kong I wrote to her from the top of Victoria Peak. I wrote to her from a small room on Koh San Road in Bangkok. In Kuala Lumpur I wrote to her from a Hindu temple built under the open canopy of the Batu Caves. I wrote to her from a small Malaysian village in the middle of a rubber-tree forest. I wrote to her from the shore of the Arabian Sea in Bombay and from the zoo in Berlin. In Leningrad I wrote to her from the nave of an Orthodox church. At a dacha somewhere outside Leningrad, I wrote to her from a wedding party. I wrote to her from Moscow and Kiev and Tbilisi and Samarqand. In Tashkent, I scribbled notes to her from the fortress of Ghengis Khan. And on an overnight train from Bavaria to Paris, I sat up all night in my berth and only then wondered what I could possibly expect from her. I knew what I wanted—I wanted her love. I wanted her acceptance. At the very least, I wanted her to be impressed by my effort. After all, not since the simpleton Candide went off in search of Cunégonde had I known of anyone going on such a picaresque in pursuit of love.

Apparently, a circumnavigation of the globe in the name of love didn't carry the same cachet for me as it did for Voltaire's imaginary lovers. While I was off sleeping in third-class railcars with livestock and spending time with men with guns, Laura had fallen in love with a nine-foot-tall Belgian basketball player with hands the size of my torso—an eventuality I should have been better prepared for, but wasn't. All I could do was make feeble attempts to woo her away from her *Übermensch*. I met her for long walks and long coffees and told her my long stories. I read my letters to her, episodically, stretching them out over as many days as possible. In the end, she was flattered by my intentions, which were obvious. She was intrigued by my stories. She was engaged by my company, or so I like to think. But that was the extent of it. She was in love with the giant. I stuck around for a few months, waiting and hoping that she would consider a smaller man. We did spend quite a few nights together. However, the closer we came to the intimacy we'd shared that summer in Berkeley and in our letters afterward, the more she started to distance herself. And then one night on the metro, on the way to a party, she turned me away completely. She made it clear that I was irritating her and that I had no place in her world. She was very convincing, and I had no choice but to believe her. I stayed away after that, but still waited. I waited a few weeks, and when I didn't hear from Laura, I made a quiet exit, returning to Los Angeles.

2. Vivian (1991–94)

How do I explain Vivian? The only way to explain Vivian is to say that someone had to follow Laura. My life had to be lived. I needed to live and not think. And then, in the vast expanse of L.A., along came Vivian, who was more than willing to help me accomplish this goal.

Unlike Laura, Vivian was a sizable woman with large appetites. She had big tits, wide hips, a round ass, and strong thighs. She loved to eat, she loved to smoke, and she was savage in the sack. She slept with men, she slept with women, her sexual energy was irrepressible. There would be no traveling around the world for her. There would be no frustrated nights politely talking around sex. In fact, on our first night together, she threw me down on her bed and we went at it and, then, went at it some more. We had so much sex that night, I was sexed-out for days afterward. Thus, Vivian became that someone. We dated for a while, if you can call it that, and then, several months later, as our relationship made me realize how lonely I had become after a year of traveling on my own, after a year composed largely of brief encounters, I took up Vivian's offer to move in with her and her feral cat, Gladys.

I packed up my small, unfurnished studio along the Miracle Mile and added my belongings to hers in her slightly larger and well-furnished studio in the Guatemalan and El Salvadoran section of Mid-Wilshire. Perhaps it was the close quarters, or that we were both too young, perhaps Vivian was too much woman for me to handle, but as soon as I gave up my apartment, our relationship took on an edge. Within the first month of our cohabitation, we each developed new, disturbing personalities, and this life of mine of living without much consideration for common sense was off and running. Thrown out of my head were the cautionary tales of the wayward women who slept on my mother's couch. If this was love, I was ready to bark and howl.

We started gnawing away at all the little things we couldn't stand about each other, all the little things that we wished we could change. And from there, we quickly moved into all the vital fears that existed at the core of our relationship. She feared that I was trying to undermine and dismantle her independence and ambition. I feared that she was trying to undermine and dismantle my codependence and lack of ambition. She feared the idealized love that I had felt for Laura. I feared her large stable of male and female ex-lovers who called all the time. She feared I would be unable to continue loving a woman who binged on food and cigarettes in the middle of the night. I feared she wouldn't continue loving a man who figured he would commit suicide when he'd had enough. We were in trouble, but we weren't willing to give up quite just yet. Given our mutual self-hatred and the parity of anger we felt for the world, it was a distinct possibility (in my mind at least) that we were ideal mates. We both thought, for whatever reason, that the fights might subside if we moved into a larger apartment.

We moved into a sizable one-bedroom Spanish colonial revival in Silverlake, which Vivian—an accomplished collector of art and vintage furniture and antiques—turned into a small paradise. There wasn't a corner or window ledge or empty wall for which she couldn't find just the right statuette or fruit-crate label or painting. And sure enough, for a few months at any rate, we were looking good in our substantially larger and well-ordered space. Behaving ourselves nicely. But soon the fights started up again and intensified and became increasingly hateful and violent, as if we were making up for the time we had been living quietly.

It got so bad—the sick enjoyment we each took away from this receiving and inflicting of pain—that I thought about returning to smaller dimensions, to the cramped and alienated quarters we'd lived in when we'd first met. But, the thing was, I was afraid. As much as I feared being the mongrel hound that I had undeniably become, I feared myself. I feared being alone. Under the right circumstances, Los Angeles alienation can be blissful; late at night, a drive along Mulholland or Sunset or Pacific Coast Highway is meditative and calming and easily floats you along. Too much alienation—the kind of dose that I had taken before I met Vivian— intensifies the pull of gravity. I was afraid of getting dragged under, and I think Vivian was as well. Although it wasn't spoken, we tacitly agreed that to drag each other down was more attractive than doing it all on our own. And so, we stuck. And slowly our urban, middle-class trappings that we had grown accustomed to became the stage on which we lost our minds and learned to love to despise each other.

I'm proud to say that although it took a great deal of restraint, I never laid a hand on Vivian. She, on the other hand, if she had been a man or a more muscular woman, would have been a good candidate for a restraining order. When she was angry, she raged. And when she was raging, she couldn't help herself: she liked to kick and slap and punch, and if something within reach wasn't of great sentimental or monetary value, she would throw it at me or smash it down on our nice kitchen tile. In keeping with her vintage aesthetic and her East Coast WASP upbringing, dishware and glass tumblers and, on occasion, an ashtray were her weapons of choice. To her credit, she never bit, she never lunged at me with a knife, she never tried to strangle me in my sleep. She enjoyed screaming and pushing over furniture. Her favorite thing to do was to lock me out of the apartment and shut off the lights.

Our fights lasted for days, if not weeks, at a time, until something would click inside our heads, and it would be time to fuck. We fucked, we fucked, we fucked, we fucked to the point of weeping. Then we fought. Over three years, the longest cease-fire, I think, was a month. And that was only because Vivian was out of town doing fieldwork. Our fights, if you are of a certain mind, could be considered darkly comic. If you're not of that mind, well, they were basically sick and twisted. I, for one, shifted back and forth between perceiving them as humorous and psychotic. Humorous or psychotic? You be the judge:

- The time she invited the young Frenchwoman Marianne to stay with us for a month. Vivian fell in love with her and, over coffee one day, told her as much. When Marianne didn't return her affection, Vivian came to our bed and told me what had happened, about the love she felt for this woman, then asked me, the man she lived with, to kick Marianne to the curb for crushing her. When I refused—I enjoyed Marianne's company—Vivian stormed out of the apartment in search of a motel and blamed me for her unhappiness.
- The day she chased me through the streets of Venice, pelting me with bagels for reasons she didn't want to explain.
- The morning she hunted me down in a full café and screamed (loudly) at me for twenty minutes for having left the apartment before we could resolve a fight that had already lasted for three days.
- The night I had taken her out to an expensive restaurant for her birthday and made the mistake of reaching across the table with my fork to taste her appetizer. She stormed out and disappeared.
- The time she slept with an ex-boyfriend because I had agreed to let her visit him in San Francisco. Apparently, trusting her enough to visit her ex-boyfriend meant that I didn't love her. She delivered this news as we were having sex.

Sick and twisted eventually won. On the stoop of a friend's apartment building, when taking a break from a weeklong domestic battle, I had all the symptoms of a heart attack. My friend drove me to the emergency room, where I was diagnosed with pleurisy, an inflammation, or blistering, of the lungs, a breathless condition that makes you feel as if your head is completely detached from your shoulders and your lungs have been shrink-wrapped. The ailment, which to the best of my knowledge only exists in the works of Dostoyevsky, is brought on by stress and is often accompanied by an acute anxiety attack.

Vivian, it was clear, was winning the war.

I'd had enough. I wanted out. But, my God, you can't imagine how sick I was. As much as I wanted out, I wanted more. I wanted this thing to go on forever. It had been three years since Vivian and I had first met and started in on this business. Three years of near strangulations and adrenal nights, nights of barking the most horrible things at each other. We dug into the most fragile parts of who we were and viciously clawed away. The amazing thing was, once we had exhausted the discourse, once all the screaming was over, once we had cleaned up all the broken dishes and tumblers and ashtrays, the sex was fantastic. The longer we fought, the better the sex. The better the sex, the longer the cease-fire. The longer the cease-fire, the bigger the next fight and the better the sex. This was our cycle of eternal returns.

"Where is this going?" we always asked each other at the end of our conflicts. "This can't go on," we'd say as if we were in the mind of Beckett. "Or can it?" And then came the sex. *This*—aside from a monotonous job I had taken in the antiseptic offices of a corporate law firm—was my life. *This* was what I was now living for. No longer was I thinking about the novel I had been writing. I no longer spent time with my friends—they couldn't stomach seeing me so fucked-up. I wanted more of *this*! I wanted more fights. More savage sex. I wanted to shorten my existence. I wanted to be sent back to the emergency room for more oxygen.

And then came along the first of two deus ex machinas that would shape the cinematic "arc" of my life. Out of the rusty L.A. sky, there it was, an unmistakable divergence from the loop-de-loop Vivian and I had been on. After years of struggling to find a meaningful position, Vivian was offered a job at the Fresno Cultural Exchange, whose offices were located, naturally, in Fresno.

Fresno, the one place where never in a million years could I ever imagine living. Fresno, where my Korean mechanic, who moonlighted as a bounty hunter, went searching for human game with his .357 Magnum. She offered to stay. I encouraged her to go. She asked me to join her. I said no. I was strong. I wasn't going to give in. No, I said, and went so far as to drive up to Fresno to help her find a house. And as a testament to my strength, I still didn't give in.

We packed up the apartment, rented a U-Haul, and resettled her and my good friend Gladys the cat. I moved into the breakfast nook of an overly populated apartment just off La Brea and Beverly. The good news was that Vivian, in our separation, took all of the furniture and all of the beautiful things she had acquired, so it wasn't a problem for me to fit into my cozy living space. After three years of material comfort, I was back where I'd started. I missed all the creature comforts that I knew I would miss, and all of the fears I'd had about being alone were realized. In no time, I was suffering from Vivian withdrawals. I wasn't so much missing Vivian as I was missing the whole smorgasbord of destruction. I have no rational explanation for this, but I wanted her back. I didn't want to be alone sleeping in a fetal position in a cramped breakfast nook. I didn't want to be single in the vast megalopolis of Los Angeles. I was ready to move to Fresno. I was ready to join my mechanic in business and take up bounty hunting.

On her next visit to L.A., we spent a marvelous weekend fighting and having sex, at which point I did something that only proved to anyone who knew me that I had, indeed, lost my mind: I asked Vivian to marry me. It wasn't well thought out or planned. It just came out in the middle of a flare-up. Posed, more than proposed, as a challenge: to live together, sick and twisted, until one of us committed murder. Out of politeness, she said she would have to consider my proposal.

On the phone the next day, she called to tell me that she had met someone, a fifty-year-old Mexican-American, Vietnam-vet sculptor. All of the things that I hated about her, she said, he loved. And she, in return, loved him for it. Go on, I said. Go be with your fifty-year-old Mexican-American, Vietnam-vet sculptor.

I drank continuously for two weeks, until late one night, lit on three bottles of red wine, I drove out onto Interstate 5, into the first torrential rain of the season, without windshield wipers. I made it to the outskirts of East L.A., where I swerved to the side of the road and spent most of the night waiting for the kaleidoscopic effect of the rain to subside. I crept into my breakfast nook at five in the morning, slept for an hour, and still drunk, went off again, keeping myself awake by chain-smoking all the way to Fresno. I knocked on Vivian's door when I arrived. She wouldn't let me in. Go home, she said. I went to a pay phone and called her repeatedly until she picked up. She told me to check myself into the Motel 6 on Olive and meet her across the street at George's for some Armenian shish kebab.

I was shaking when she turned up an hour later. The second I saw Vivian, I knew I truly couldn't stand this woman. I hated this woman. I despised her. Just the sight of her disgusted me. I thought, What am I doing here? At which point, I realized, it was *me. I* was the lost one. *I* was the crazy one. I wasn't disgusted by her, I was disgusted with myself. There she was, starting her career, starting fresh with a friendly and probably well-armed father figure, and I had become nothing more than what we'd been for the last three years—one of two bickering people. Only now I was alone, bickering with myself, eating myself alive. What had I done? What had I turned into? Had I taken all the passion that I felt toward Laura and applied it to my relationship with Vivian? Did I hold on for as long as I did because I was determined to make things work, or was it because I had become addicted to receiving and inflicting pain? Whatever I had become, I didn't like it. For so long my anger had been directed inward. What would become of me now that I'd let it become unleashed?

We got drunk. We forced ourselves to say some kind words, such as "It wasn't all bad," "We did have some good times," and we were agreed that we would both miss the sex. The following morning we shared a muffin and coffee and I walked away crying, a weeping spectacle for Fresno passersby. I was spent. To this day, I have never been so spent. And I hadn't yet realized it, but that day was the first day of a two-month-long nervous breakdown. The following morning I showed up for work at the law offices of Sidley & Austin, sat at my desk in front of a pile of EPA studies on toxic frogs, and for hours stared into a blank computer monitor. I was near catatonic until I was shaken awake by my supervisor. Without a word, I stood up, walked away from her, and went home. I bought an airline ticket for Miami the following morning—after fourteen years of being alone, my mother had found a man worthy of her, and from the time I arrived at my mother and stepfather's house in Coral Gables, I slept, I smoked, I drank, I cried, I watched TV.

I waited.

3. Christine (1994–)

Where Christine and I met is the least interesting part of our story. When I think of our first meeting, and then the years of friendship that followed, I don't like to think of our initial impressions being formed there in that white room with no windows surrounded by lifeless and hollow faces. I prefer not to think of us vista-less, contained on the forty-eighth floor of a glass and steel structure, but rather, sitting outdoors, somewhere with a view of the sky and the ocean, in all those beautiful places from which I used to write letters to Laura. If I had the power to replay those years, if I were writing a fiction, I would choose to set our long, late-night talks on a bench overlooking Pacific Coast Highway. A persistent crash of waves in the distance. Desert heat blowing in from the Mojave. This place, these details, would better suit the story, but I suppose it doesn't really matter where we were when we met and grew on each other—even if it was there, in our small internal compartment, surrounded by bored and idle faces and the glow of computer monitors and the hum of circuitry. The important thing was that she was there.

Christine was blond—a true blond, a real California blond, a seventh-generation California blond—and thin, with big blue eyes and a wide Scandinavian face. Essentially, a California classic, the physical type the world associates with the American West. Her hair hung straight to the small of her back, her voice was girlish, she was charmingly clumsy, and she tended to mispronounce words in a comically uninhibited way. She had been living in cities for the past ten years, but belying her fashion and her interests in sophisticated art and music and exotic, far-flung places, it was obvious that she'd originated from somewhere more earthy and animistic. She was born and raised in the Central Valley, but wasn't from the Valley itself, but rather from the Sierra Nevada, where she lived on a mountaintop with her four siblings and her horse and some livestock, and where, as a child, she sang Don Ho's "Tiny Bubbles" to the drunk guests at her parents' mountaintop resort. Her uncles and cousins, like those generations of Californians before them, were farmers and cowboys; she, herself, raised pigs and was at one time a Future Farmer of America.

For almost two years before Vivian and I split up, Christine and I had lunch together at least twice a week, during which time Christine took it upon herself to console me and cheer me up, to treat me as she would a wounded animal. She was good at this, tending to my wounds. She had an easiness about her, a gentle way of grounding me into the world of the living. But as sweet as she appeared, she wasn't faint of heart. Although she didn't have many complaints of her own, she could sit across from me for hours at a time and laugh at me and all my seething bitterness. For hours, as if

71

it were merely a passing fog, she could genially smile at the miasma of my dark fatalism and overblown sense of futility.

We were obviously taken with each other, Christine and I, but other than subtle innuendo and a little flirtation, we never talked about what was obvious. We did, however, have a friendly date one weekend afternoon when Vivian was away in Phoenix for that peaceful monthlong respite of ours. We took in a Mexican movie, *Like Water for Chocolate*, a sexy, tongue-in-cheek tragic comedy, based on the book by the same title, which involved a great deal of sensual food preparation and bodice ripping and lovemaking and family curses and magic spells. We were both a little turned on, I think, by all the hot chili peppers and the breast sweat dripping into the mole sauce. We were also a little hungry and so had a meal at El Coyote afterward, where, under glowing chili pepper lights and beside a booth full of Elvis impersonators, Christine told me the story about how she ended up in Los Angeles, at which point I understood why, for the moment, she tolerated my endless talk about my domestic nightmare.

While she was living in San Francisco, Christine had met Sam, a nice Jewish boy and recovering heroin addict who had a penchant for sleeping with Hollywood Boulevard prostitutes. Sam, who lived in L.A. and who worked as a music producer, fell for Christine and spent the better part of six months wooing her with long letters and surprise visits. So wooing was Sam that he convinced Christine to move down south to be with him. They found an apartment together in Hollywood. She found a job and enrolled at Otis Parsons to study fabric design, and they lived happily for six months—until, that is, Sam one day started openly showing affection to one of the neighbors. His behavior grew increasingly disrespectful and sadistic, and Christine, who felt as though she had been bamboozled, grew increasingly frustrated.

One night as she was baking a cake for a colleague who was

taking maternity leave, as she was stirring the batter of this cake intended for her pregnant friend, all the bad feelings that she felt for Sam were stirring inside her. The more she stirred, the worse she felt. She poured the batter into the pan, put it in the oven, closed the oven door, and removed the cake forty minutes later to find that it hadn't risen. Its center was concave, its edges lumpy and overly crisp. It was ugly. It was, in fact, the ugliest cake Christine—who prided herself on her baked goods—had ever baked. Nevertheless, she iced the cake and took it to the party, but no one touched it. They looked it over; they looked it over sadly. That night, she returned home with her sad, untouched cake and told Sam to pack his things and get out. Sam packed up and left, and when he had gone, Christine cut off a small piece of the pathetic dessert and placed it in a teacup—to remind herself of how she felt, to remind her not to ever allow herself to feel this way again.

She placed the teacup on top of her refrigerator and threw the remainder of the cake in the trash. The small piece of cake in the teacup dried up, and when she moved out of the apartment she and Sam had shared, she packaged the cup, cake included, took it with her, and placed it on top of the refrigerator in her new apartment. She moved three times and each time she placed the teacup with its morsel of cake on top of the refrigerator. But for two years, I learned over dinner that night at El Coyote, as we sat under the chili-pepper glow, Sam continued to come and go, in and out of her life, in and out of her bed, raising and then diminishing expectations, and for this she felt a great deal of shame; and although this shame wasn't easy to see on someone as easygoing as Christine, it soon became evident to me that Christine was something of a wreck. No wonder she enjoyed listening to me eviscerate myself, I remember thinking—it brought her a good deal of catharsis to hear me prattle on about my own shame. Still, I told her that I didn't think she should be ashamed. I admired her for being smart enough to throw him out. I admired her for knowing what she could and couldn't put up with. I was sure she would know when to cut him off completely.

When I returned from Miami after my period of convalescence, I still had to wake up in the morning and take hot baths and chant and breathe to relieve the pressure before I could start the day. Although I was no longer suicidal, I was still in great pain, but when I would see Christine at work, the pain would ease. Her presence soothed it. I told her as much, and we started spending time together on the outside. Almost every night, she would visit my apartment on Detroit Street or I would visit her small apartment in Los Feliz, and we would sit around drinking tea and talking and laughing late into the night, and on at least one or two occasions when she wasn't looking, I went to her refrigerator and looked inside the teacup. I held it in my hands and thought about what it meant to her, and I wondered if Sam had been around lately.

We managed to last for a month before we had our first kiss. The kiss, which was made at the door, hesitantly, as if it were a great danger, was received well by both of us and led to more kisses, and then to bed. In the morning it was evident on her face that she was afraid of me, and I, seeing her afraid, was made equally afraid. I knew now that romantic intentions didn't really sort out until there was a feeling of security, and until then, who knew what a person was made of?

I was still ailing, but I decided to believe that whatever this was going to be, should it continue or end, would continue or end amicably. We were agreed, Christine and I, not to talk about feelings until we were absolutely solid. We were agreed that we would be gentle with each other. We were agreed that we wouldn't bicker or fight. I'm fond of you, I would say. I'm fond of you, she would say. And we left it at that and stuck to it.

And then came the second deus ex machina, only this one felt more like an act of divine intervention. And with it, came a little salvation for two damaged people.

Three weeks after we had consummated our friendship, Christine took a trip to San Francisco. I drove her to the airport on a Thursday and I remember feeling happy for the first time in years when I said good-bye to her. Genuinely happy and hopeful and alive. I had started writing applications to graduate schools. I was back to work on my book. I had taken a few extra jobs and had a little money. A bedroom had opened up in the apartment—no longer was I living in the breakfast nook. And my roommates turned-out to be loving men who, along with Christine, helped nurse me back to health. A few days later, early in the morning of January 17, 1994, the fates served up an earthquake in Northridge that measured 7.2 on the Richter scale. I was catapulted out of bed and thrown across the room. An electric transformer blew up outside my window. The flash from the explosion blinded me. The building shook so violently, I felt as if I were in a blender. I could hear the timber behind the stucco walls rattling, trying to decide whether to give up or hold strong. I tried to stand in the doorway, but the door had slammed shut and something had fallen in its path. It wouldn't budge. All I could do was hold on to the knob and pray nothing crashed into my skull.

The earthquake only shook for a short time, but as they say when such things happen, it felt as if it would never end. When everything was finally still, I managed to get the door open. Brian and Andrew, the men I lived with, found a flashlight and guided me down the long hall of our apartment and led me outside. I followed the parabola of light to the street, where, for the first time in all the years I had been living under the big Los Angeles sky, as it would be in the desert or in the mountains, the sky was thick with stars. The city was blacked out and its artificial light had been replaced by the light of the cosmos. So thick was this cosmic light, you could see the gaseous haze of the Milky Way.

That night, I felt as if the universe were showing itself to me for a reason. In the presence of its awesome expanse, I felt as if the remaining undercurrent of despair I had been living with had been released from me. I stood in the middle of the street, and before I could say anything to anyone, all I could do was look up not unlike the way those bedazzled figures do in Jesus paintings. We all looked up in wonder that night, and all of us lay down on the lawn and talked under the stars until first light. And when first light came amidst aftershocks wobbling us and the cars on the roadside, we were all infected with a little bit of vertigo.

On Wednesday night, I drove to LAX to pick up Christine and drove her to Los Feliz, where along a stretch of Hollywood Boulevard a number of old brick buildings had fallen into rubble. All up and down Christine's street, people were walking with mattresses and trunks and televisions and bundles of clothes. We found a parking spot nearby and walked to her building, which, like the rest on the block, had been tagged for evacuation. Inside her apartment, the walls had cracked. A fissure had opened up wide enough so that you could see outside into the neighbor's yard. Everything had fallen out of the closets and kitchen cabinets, and on the kitchen floor was a mound of broken dishes and glass. I followed Christine around the small apartment, telling her every-thing would be all right, and found myself apologizing for the earthquake. We gathered up the things that had fallen out of the closets, righted the lamps, then went to work on the kitchen. We carefully picked at the broken glass and the ceramics and piled the pieces into a trash bag. And then, Christine gasped—she gasps when she's moved or excited. Without irony, she gasped and pointed. She pointed to the floor and said in a small voice, "The teacup." She slowly bent down and gathered what was left of it, then said, "The cake." I looked down. "Where is it?" she asked. The teacup, which was at the very bottom of the pile, must have been the first thing to have fallen when the earthquake started. There was no sign of the cake. It had been pulverized by the force of all the dishes falling out of the cabinets. It had turned to dust.

I looked at Christine. I looked at the floor. I looked at her, deep into her, and I said, "I don't think you need it anymore."

"No?" she said.

"No."

"Are you sure?"

"Yes," I said.

Christine grabbed hold of me and didn't let go. She was crying now, and laughing, and although it seems silly to place so much emphasis on an odd and idiosyncratic and sentimental object, she and I knew exactly what this meant. We both felt it. We both felt a euphoria that one feels when a course of events proves to be bigger than anything you might ever have considered. I'm not a religious person, I'm not even particularly spiritual, but I felt as if I were being guided. Here, the forces of nature were saying, Don't be a fool.

We packed her bags. We fit as much as we could into my small car, and that afternoon she moved into my small room. Over the next several days, we emptied her apartment and brought everything over. She moved in and she didn't leave. I'm fond of you, I would say for many months afterward. I'm fond of you, she would say for many months afterward. But we both knew that our feelings were far greater than what we said.

More than with anyone else in my life, Christine and I lived peacefully, and with Christine in my life, my feelings of despair and my anger were still there, but they were somehow easier to live with. I could just look at Christine and know that if she could love me, I couldn't be all that awful.

The following summer, we were married in Bedford Corners, New York, by a rabbi with a Beatles bowl-cut. Four years later, Alexander Peterson Grand and Nathanael Peterson Grand, fraternal twins, were born. Their grandfather, my father, who still lives in Queens—only twenty minutes away from our Brooklyn apartment—has never met them and probably never will. The boys,

77

who will be five this year, have started to ask about him. I still haven't figured out how to explain how a man could be so prideful and destructive to throw away his own family. After all these years, it still makes as little sense to me as it did when I was a kid.

What I am sure of, what makes absolute sense, is that with Christine in my life I have been granted the freedom to learn what it means to be a man.

The Five Stages of Marriage

ANDY BOROWITZ

Marriage be not proud, though some have called thee mighty and dreadful.

—John Donne (1572–1631)

A wise man once said that marriage is something that will happen to all of us sooner or later, whether we like it or not. Moments after making that observation, the wise man—on the eve of his own wedding, to which 250 guests had been invited and for which a nine-thousand-dollar deposit had already been made to the caterers—threw himself under the wheels of a hurtling city bus and was instantly squished. But the wise man's act, while admittedly rash, does little to diminish the essential wisdom of his observation about the inexorable nature of marriage. If anything, it may make him seem even wiser, except perhaps to the bride's family, who to this day still refer to him as "that worthless *douchebag*."

Like that wise man, each of us knows on some level that marriage is inevitable, but unlike him, we choose not to dwell on such an unpleasant fact, preferring instead to live our lives as if marriage did not exist. Well practiced in the art of self-deception, we sweep marriage into the far corners of our minds, crowding it out with thoughts of NASCAR, the World Wrestling Federation, and Angelina Jolie. But try as we might to pretend otherwise, marriage waits for each and every one us like an unwanted party guest, brandishing its awful scythe, ready to hack us limb from limb before it is our time. Attempting to live our lives as if marriage will never hunt us down is a tempting strategy but, at the end of the day, pure folly. Marriage will find all of us eventually, just as molten lava found each and every citizen of Pompeii.

In earlier, "primitive" societies, religious rituals and ceremonies helped the male members of a tribe navigate the treacherous journey into marriage, which they generally viewed as a mysterious realm from which there was no possibility of return. Before one could enter this terrifying realm, a trip that inspired no small measure of dread, one's soul had to be elaborately prepared for safe passage. Often a tribal witch doctor or shaman would perform an elaborate rite in which a man about to be married had all traces of hope exorcised from his being. Once his spirit had thoroughly been extinguished, the bridegroom would be smeared with the blood of a dead and therefore hopeless animal or festooned with the feathers of a clinically depressed bird to make his transition to "the other side" smooth, much as the groom of today rents a tuxedo. It is tempting to conclude that these ancient customs helped ease the bachelor's path to marriage in ways that our modern, more secular rituals of hiring strippers and drinking with college roommates until we vomit on each other do not. And yet, much evidence suggests that our tribal forefathers, for all of their blood-smearing and feather-festooning, were just as creeped out by marriage as we, their fucked-up descendants, are today. Cave drawings in Malaysia dating to the fourth century BC, showing newly married men hurling their bodies off a cliff, seem to confirm the view that even centuries before the invention of the city bus, marriage was viewed much as it is today: something to be feared, avoided, and escaped at all costs.

Marriage takes some men when they are young, at a time when they might otherwise assume, rightly or not, that they have their whole lives ahead of them. For these men, cut down in the prime of their lives by a sudden, unwanted wedding, the institution of matrimony may seem arbitrary and unfair, a cruel joke perpetrated on them by the random forces of a godless universe. "I'm too young to be married," these men will cry, clutching the latest issue of *Maxim, FHM,* or *Stuff,* wondering, with some justification, "Why me?" And yet, it is safe to say that no matter how old one is, at no time of life is a man truly "ready" to be married. A man who marries later in life, in fact, may find his matrimonial experience even more unsettling and calamitous than he would have had he married earlier, since he has had more years to lull himself into the delusion that marriage was a noose he could somehow slip. Regardless of one's age, however, no man loses his bachelor status without profound suffering—emotional, mental, and even physical—a state of affairs that the so-called coping professions, until quite recently, have regrettably chosen to ignore.

Case in point: if one visits the Marriage and Marrying section of one's local bookstore, one will immediately be struck by the dearth of truly helpful titles aimed at the man who is in the throes of marriage and is fighting for his very survival. Most of these self-help tomes are penned by abject charlatans, offering little more than vacuous cheerleading as they attempt to persuade us that marriage, if viewed from the proper perspective, can bring a greater, deeper meaning to the very life that it is tirelessly snuffing out. Many of these bogus volumes include first-person narratives of "near-marriage" experiences, related by men who came close to being married but rallied at the last moment and lived to tell the tale. These stories, with their obligatory claims of men having seen a "white light" at the end of a "long tunnel," serve up a pseudo-supernatural take on marriage that may be comforting, but that is ultimately of little real value. In point of fact, most medical professionals now believe that the oft-mentioned "long tunnel" reported by the almost-married may merely be the center aisle of the church or synagogue where the wedding was to have taken place, and that the "white light" is nothing more than the bride's wedding dress, seen in a blur before the groom passed out, ran out of the wedding, or suffered a psychotic break. Given that such near-marriage stories have been so widely discredited, it is a scandal that publishers continue to foist them on an unsuspecting public. But the very fact of their publication raises a larger question: Do books that attempt to offer falsely soothing perspectives on marriage serve any public good at all?

As a clinical psychologist, I firmly believe the answer is no. I know I will win no popularity contests by stating the true, unvarnished facts about marriage, but state them I must: in the last calendar year alone, marriage took the lives of more men than cancer, heart disease, and mine cave-ins combined. Sobering statistics like these are part of the reason that I have dedicated my life's work to making men's experience with marriage and marrying, if not survivable, then at least marginally less traumatic. A lofty pursuit, some might say, but one that has given me tremendous personal satisfaction and that will someday, God willing, provide me with a book deal of my very own.

In the fall of 1997, along with the award-winning clinical psychologists Dr. Hugo Freisch of the University of Berlin and Dr. Marianne Kronholz of the University of Stuttgart, I founded the Institute for the Study of Marriage and Marrying in a leafy suburb of Hartford, Connecticut. Working out of a storefront that had once belonged to the Tanfastic Tanning Salon, Drs. Freisch, Kronholz, and I set for ourselves what in retrospect must have seemed to our peers in the scientific community to be a ludicrously ambitious, even hubristic goal: to study the long-term emotional, psychological, and physical effects of marriage on men who, through no fault of their own, suddenly find themselves married.

It was not easy finding patients willing to open up about marriage. Matrimony, it seems, is the final taboo in our society, something everyone must eventually deal with and yet no one wants to discuss, even at gunpoint. It is a shopworn cliché that there are only two sure things in this life—marriage and taxes—and yet, judging from the steady stream of customers who daily poured into the H & R Block office next door to the institute, people seemed much more inclined to talk about their taxes than about their marriages. Discussing the "marriage penalty" with their accountants was, apparently, as close to discussing marriage as many of these people were willing to do—even though the penalties that marriage imposes on the core of a man's very being are so much more acute and punishing than those inflicted on his wallet, which, by the way, are also pretty bad.

On weekends, Drs. Freisch, Kronholz, and I frequented the places where we were most likely to find married men—hardware stores, sports bars, and Circuit City stores. And find them we did: hollow-eyed and desperate, wandering about in a kind of self-imposed purgatory, listlessly inspecting DVD players or ordering plates of loaded nachos, looking for any excuse not to return home. Eventually, with promises of generous cash payments and a keg of Miller genuine draft, we induced them to come back with us to the institute and talk about what marriage had done to them. After interviewing hundreds of such men, Drs. Freisch and Kronholz and I made an amazing discovery: with few exceptions, the men's responses to their marriages followed an identical pattern, which could be broken down into five distinct and identifiable phases. The following, then, is a summary of those phases, which we have come to call the Five Stages of Marriage.

Stage One: Denial

In the first stage, denial, the newly married man reacts to his altered marital status with total and unyielding disbelief. While in this stage, which often lasts for months, years, or in some rare cases decades, the married man will vehemently refute any suggestion that he has "tied the knot" and will routinely mark the box labeled

SINGLE on tax forms, driver's license applications, and the like. A man in the denial stage may even attempt to "externalize" his behavior by arguing that the woman who persists in calling herself his wife is a pathological liar, raving lunatic, or scam artist. As bizarre as his behavior may sound, most psychologists now agree that denial is a near-universal first response to being married, common in over ninety-eight percent of the married male population. And far from being damaging or unhealthy, denial may in fact be the most adaptive reaction one can have to the initial horror of learning that one is no longer single.

David G. woke up one morning and was alarmed to see a strange woman in his bed. Bolting upright, he shouted, "Who the hell are you?" When the still-groggy woman explained that she was David's wife, Katie, David would have none of it, demanding that the woman leave his house at once. Eventually, Katie called the police and David was carted off to a psychiatric ward for evaluation. The six months that David spent institutionalized served an invaluable role in riding out the first stage of marriage, which is often the most problematic. That Katie divorced him during his convalescence and moved back with her parents in Denver is worth noting, but ultimately is of little or no pertinence to the larger issues of our research.

Stage Two: Anger

Stage one, denial, is widely considered a day at the beach compared to stage two, anger. Once denial has worn off, the married man is left with no protective armor to shield himself from the dawning of the horrifying revelation that he is, in fact, married, and there is not a fucking thing he can do about it. In our interviews with men, Drs. Freisch, Kronholz, and I came to call this the "Why me?" phase, since "Why me?" was the question our interviewees most often asked, with "Is there anything left in that keg?" a close second.

As the reality of the married man's terrible situation becomes thoroughly undeniable, he will express anger at his marital status and will lash out at people he deems appropriate targets, in most cases single friends who have not made the same idiotic mistake he has. Jeffrey H. spent most of the late 1990s in such an angry phase, using his every spare moment to make harassing phone calls to single friends of his who were white-water rafting, motorcycling across the country, or just hanging out in their underwear on Sunday mornings, activities that for married men are strictly things of the past. After his friends started changing their cell phone numbers, one by one, he started vandalizing their apartments. Jeffrey H. was picked up by the police while spray-painting the words BLOW ME on the home of a college roommate in Orlando and later spent six months in an institution—a period that he now sees as time well spent.

Stage Three: Bargaining

In the third stage, bargaining, the married man attempts to cut a number of deals or "bargains" to lessen the pain of being married. The bargaining phase represents a positive step in the married man's engagement with his marriage, because unlike stage one and two, in stage three he is actually speaking to his wife.

"I'll tell you what," Roger K. remembers telling his wife, Brenda. "I'll clean out the garage, take out the trash every day, and even do the grocery shopping for you." "Okay," a skeptical Brenda replied, "but what's the catch?" At that point, Roger revealed the true nature of his "bargain": "You have to go away forever."

Brenda, not surprisingly, refused. Roger then changed the terms of the bargain, asking Brenda to go away for five years, then three years, then two weeks. Ultimately, he begged her to leave for an hour. Brenda, unyielding, refused to bite, instead unleashing a torrent of tears, which forced Roger to hold up his end of the bargain while gaining nothing in return. Despondent at this un-fortunate turn of events, Roger turned to religion, a not-infrequent occurrence during the bargaining stage. He started praying three times a day, asking the Almighty to make Brenda vanish, or at the very least turn into a pillar of salt. During the fifth day of such religious observances, Brenda found Roger on the knees of their bedroom bellowing, "O God, dear God, just make her go away!" She demanded that he seek emergency psychiatric care, and while Roger today says that the six months he spent in an institution were not the bargain he had been seeking, they were, in his words, "better than a poke in the eye with a sharp stick."

Stage Four: Depression

When bargaining fails—and in marriage, it always does—the man is left with a profound sense of loss, hopelessness, and despair. He no longer engages in the manic behavior that characterizes the bargaining phase. He no longer rereads the wedding vows over and over in the vain search for a "loophole." He is, in a word, defeated. His depression may take two forms: "reactive depression," re-sponding to the years of marriage that have already gone down the tubes, and "preparatory depression," suffering in anticipation of the terrifying, yawning chasm of time that his future married life now represents.

Stage four is often seen as the most intractable of the five stages, and the one that demands the most energy and inventiveness from the married man's caregivers. Hoping that the married man will eventually "get over it" or "cheer up" is not an option, since depression over one's marital status has been observed to be among the most tenacious and virulent depressions documented in the medical literature. During this stage, role-playing games have been shown to be helpful in getting the depressed subject to get "out of himself"; in particular, many married men have succeeded in overcoming marital depression by taking part, every weekend, in Civil War reenactments.

Brandon Q., who had been suffering from stage-four depression for the better part of his thirties, found that donning a Union soldier's costume and rifle and engaging in mock battles helped him get his mind off his being, alas, married and that this was unlikely to change at any point in the future. On the downside, after two years of steady participation in such reenactments, Brandon attempted to set fire to the city of Atlanta. Still, Brandon believes that his brief attempt at arson, which landed him in a mental institution for six months, was helpful in overcoming his depression. "I'll do it again when I get out of here," he says today.

Stage Five: Acceptance

The fifth and final stage of marriage, acceptance, can only be achieved if the married man has been permitted to pass through each of the previous four stages and is now ready—or, as ready as he will ever be—to come to terms with marriage. Denial, anger, and depression are gone, and the only bargaining the married man may engage in is relatively harmless, such as "Can I please watch the Super Bowl if I promise we'll visit your mother next weekend?" The acceptance stage is marked by noticeable changes in the married man's demeanor: no longer agitated or upset, he is now aloof and even, perhaps, catatonic, as if the life force had been drained from him once and for all. At this point, having abandoned all hope of a miraculous reprieve, the man is prepared to make the final transition to marriage. Quiet companionship and simple activities such as basket-weaving and being wheeled around the grounds may help make this final stage of marriage as comfortable as possible, which is to say, not very.

One final note: in the interest of full disclosure, it is my regrettable duty to report that after completing our research, Dr. Freisch and Dr. Kronholz, who had been married for sixty years, divorced, citing "irreconcilable differences." Their differences, in short, were these: Dr. Kronholz thought that stage four should actually be called stage two, and vice versa, while Dr. Freisch believed that Dr. Kronholz should go to hell. Their personal woes aside, they are both consummate professionals and I wish them well.

Betting on the Come

JAMES MCMANUS

Century-class game theorists like Phil Ivey, "Manhattan Johnny" von Neumann, Richard Nixon, and "Texas Dolly" Brunson tell us we'll never be dealt enough strong cards to win money at poker in the long—or even medium—term. We therefore need to steal a few more than our fair share of pots while holding less than premium hands. More conservative pokeraticians, such as Mason Malmuth and David Sklansky, insist that players who rely too often on stone-cold bluffs (betting with nothing, hoping their opponents will fold) will go broke in a hurry, though as Cool Hand Luke handsomely drawled, "Sometimes nuthin's a pretty cool hand." A more profitable tactic is the semibluff: to bet or raise with a hand that probably isn't the best hand at the moment, such as a flush draw (four clubs, for example), but which has a reasonable shot at becoming the best hand—a flush. It's also called *betting on the come* or *bluffing with outs.* With two more cards to be dealt, you have the other nine clubs times two chances (for eighteen outs) to hit the flush, while hoping the board doesn't pair. (If it did, your opponent might have a full house, which of course beats a flush.) A semibluff thus gives you two ways to win a nice pot: hitting your flush or making your opponent fold her often superior hand.

The problem is that even the experts don't agree on the optimum frequency for deploying this tactic. If you're good, you can do it by feel: relying on gut reactions, making ad hoc decisions based on myriad clues picked up at the table, reveling in the shuffle's built-in uncertainty. You can trust in karma or guardian angels, change hats, finger heirlooms or talismans, or make more unkeepable promises to the Royal Hibernian poker gods. You can also let the cool random tao of the shuffle determine how often you do it.

When playing no-limit hold'em, I like to semibluff each time I peer between my knuckles and find either 9–8 suited or A–3 suited. My wife Jennifer and I met in 1989, and our first child was born in '98. March 1 is Jennifer's birthday. The positive associations I have with these hands make it easier for me to appear confident to opponents trying to read my face or body language as we stare each other down over strewn heaps of black and purple chips, sometimes even a couple of red-white-and-blue $5,000 Bellagio chips, nick- named *flags*. The red-and-white $25,000s are called *pancakes* (as in *these boys are flippin' 'em around like they're pancakes;* as in *win a potful, buy a house with*), but I've never played a pot with one in it. Like most married guys, I'm a sentimental fool *and* a gambler, so I'm especially keen on 9–8 and A–3 when they're suited in hearts.

And like most Americans my age—I was born in '51—I'm on my second marriage. And my last, I would hope. In fact, let me substitute *in* as the rosier preposition, smacking less of the stopgap. I'm also a typical baby boomer in that I got married too young the first time, to a person I wasn't all that compatible with. Jennifer made a similar blunder herself, though she stayed married for only about a year. She and her first husband didn't have a child, perhaps the main reason their divorce was so friendly. Mine, after thirteen years and two children, was more of a dirty bomb, cesium–137 sculpted around old-fashioned dynamite, perfectly designed to trigger panicked evacuation and eliminate critical infrastructure.

This time out, Jennifer and I are better fixed emotionally and financially, and that she's fifteen years younger than me feels in sync with our sociobiological clocks. Not that I ever wanted to become a parent again at the time we got married. After my first wife left me for another man in 1987, not only did my penis feel like an acorn with squirrelly toothmarks, but I was almost violently committed to not making any more children with it. I already had two and neither was terribly happy, in part because Dad didn't live with them. My talented, unlucky son, James, would develop acute schizophrenia and attempt suicide on several occasions. He died of a drug overdose in October 2001.

By the time I'd met Jennifer, in 1989, I still had hope for James, especially now that her nurturing spirit—her calm, sane, affectionate competence—had entered our lives. Jennifer and I took him on road trips out West; to Bulls games, to Springfield, to Scotland; to numerous local gymnasiums as he played for the seventh-grade traveling all-stars. In one fairly miraculous game, we watched him go off for seventeen points in a six-minute quarter: five of six threes and a breakaway layup after a steal. A hundred and thirty-six points and eight steals, I silently extrapolated, in a regulation NBA game. He was thirteen years old, five feet tall, and weighed about eighty-five pounds. There were players in the league who weighed twice that, who had hair on their forearms and calves, who shaved on a regular basis. But James could hang in with these guys. More than hang in. He usually had three or four steals and was often the game's highest scorer. That summer he and I made matching birdies across the water on the par 3 fifteenth at Peter Jans Golf Course. He also pitched a no-hitter in Little League, worked far beyond his grade level in math, and with the help of his stepfather was becoming a badass guitarist. His girlfriend was named Suzie Tingle. James was bewildered and pissed about his parents' divorce but otherwise seemed happy to be alive every minute.

Around fourteen, however, he began to gradually—then suddenly—spiral down into infernos of rage, depression, and passive-aggressive defiance. His mother and I had divorced when he was ten, and she'd remarried and had a child a few months later (repeating her pattern with me), though she and her second hus-

91

band separated soon after that. Our daughter, Bridget, four years older than James, would enter a similar tailspin, but eventually righted herself. With James, changing schools didn't work. Zoloft and Paxil and Prozac and Elavil didn't work. Tough love didn't work. New guitars didn't work, since he smashed both the instruments he received as birthday and Christmas gifts. Other sons with divorced parents had posters of Hendrix, Kurt Cobain, or Keith Richards on their walls, but James took these guys at their *word*.

I'll meet y'all in the next world, and don't be late.

I kill you, I'm not gonna crack.

Can't you see, Sister Morphine, I'm tryin' to score?

The hard-core posturing of "Voodoo Child" and *Sticky Fingers* I'd perfunctorily deployed twenty-five years earlier now was a code my son lived by—and was ready to die for. More psychiatrists entered the picture. So did police orders, trips to emergency rooms and mental health clinics (one for two years, out of state), a psychotic twenty-nine-year-old girlfriend, more attempts to harm and or kill himself. My role in his life was reduced to the desperate, humiliated wreck slumped in the corner of the ICU, the guy who pleaded with doctors, filled out insurance forms, murderously disputed with claims supervisors, reported his only son's various addresses to cops, social workers, RNs. I was gonna do my damnedest to help him any way I could for as long as it took, but under no circumstances would I voluntarily subject myself to any *new* doses of such mind-bending pain. As Raymond Carver put it while dealing with the two unhappy children of his first marriage: "I'd rather take poison than go through that again."

Which would have been just fine with Jennifer. Not long after I met her, she told me she'd lost her right ovary to a dermoid cyst five years earlier. Informed by her Memphis gynecologist that she'd never be fertile, she began, at eighteen, to make tough psychological adjustments. Though she wasn't fully aware of it, men who didn't want children—rare beasts—became more attractive to her. To the extent that I considered getting married again, I was looking for a wife who didn't want to become a mother, almost unheard of in young heterosexual women. In no small part because of these dovetailing yens, we allowed ourselves to fall in love during a trip to Donegal in the summer of 1990.

By the time we got married two years later, Western gynecology had advanced into fertile new territory. Jennifer's Chicago gynecologist performed a laparoscopy to mitigate the painful symptoms of endometriosis. She also surprised us by saying that Jennifer now had "an outside but reasonable chance" to get pregnant, if that's what she wanted. She did. More than anything, as it turned out.

This bolt from the blue stunned us into vigorous debate mode for the next seven years. I was already forty-one, forty-three, forty-five, with two adolescent children whose emotional needs were almost hilariously beyond my power to satisfy. *Nuclear family,* to me, was a joke or a sentence. With her usual patience and grace, though, Jennifer tried to persuade me that just because things had gone badly with my first wife didn't mean *we* were doomed to go there. "Ya gotta have a little faith, Jimmy."

"I know that. I want to. I do. It's just that . . ." I knew she was right in my heart and my brain, though my gut had impregnable doubts. And then there was Jennifer's gut, and her health overall. Because her doctor had also informed us that the endometriosis would be further relieved—and the risks of breast and uterine cancer reduced by a hefty percentage—if Jennifer got pregnant and nursed. So how could I bluff against that?

When I kvetched about my dilemma to, among countless others, U.S. poet laureate Mark Strand, who is six-seven and looks like a cross between Dante and Clint Eastwood, he gazed soulfully down at Jennifer while offering to stand in for me fatherhoodwise, and that by itself about settled it. Without making our decision a fait accompli, Jennifer went off the pill, cleaned up her diet, began doing yoga and taking evening-primrose oil. She wanted to be healthy and ready to go "just in case" Strand or I made a move.

In the fall of '97 she and I spent a five-week residency at the Rockefeller Foundation's Villa Serbelloni in Bellagio, Italy. Virgil and Catullus lovingly refer to the place, as do both Plinys, who had a summer home there, the Villa Pliniana, in the years just after Christ was born. The room Jennifer and I were assigned, No. 9, faces west and south, with views of the Lecco and Como arms of the lake, and of numerous alps. We were told that Jack Kennedy had one of his last presidential trysts in this room in June of '63, during a short break in a series of state visits to European capitals. Jackie had stayed home in Washington with five-year-old Caroline and two-year-old JFK Jr.

During our own romantic interlude in Room No. 9, Jennifer and I must have had twenty-five days of brisk autumn sun, which gave first the Lecco arm of the lake a blindingly platinum glitter, and then, as we got dressed for sumptuous dinners, the Como. High in the mountains that Halloween eve, with preposterously romantic moonlight ricocheting off the deepest freshwater in Europe, it finally sank in that only a bona fide fuckwad would compromise the health of his beautiful wife while depriving her of parenthood. She had, after all, saved my life by marrying me, and I knew that she'd make a great mother. As I performed my husbandly duty sans condom, however, I was hoping, like a bona fide fuckwad, that somehow it wouldn't quite take. The women on both sides of her family had serious fertility problems, and we had been warned that Jennifer heavy with child was a long shot. Even so, I was betting on the come and all-in.

When a pee test said Jennifer was pregnant and her doctor confirmed it, I pretended to be thrilled. This latest bluff involved taking credit for something I'd prayed wouldn't happen, accepting thumbs-ups and fists from my friends, and lying to my pregnant wife through the following August, when after thirty-eight hours of labor, twenty-five on the contraction-inducing drug Pitocin, Beatrice was born in the middle of an emergency C-section. Her name means "the bringer of joy," and she had. When a nurse finally handed her to me under the warming lamp, I got juiced to the point of delirium. *Wham!* When you're suddenly forced to understand that one of the best things in your life is something you've battled with all your guile and strength to head off, it shakes your self-confidence. In a good way, but still.

A similar bolt had struck me a couple of years after my first marriage had ended very, very much against my wishes. But what if I'd had a vasectomy then, as so many fathers do upon getting divorced? What if Jennifer had died or left or was unfaithful to me and, after a period of mourning, I fell in love with a woman who wanted, who *needed,* to have children with me, in spite of my imminent, or in-progress, geezerhood? Because what writer wouldn't want to join the same Geezer Dads Club that welcomes Fyodor Dostoyevsky, Saul Bellow, and Ismail the Bloodthirsty (who sired fourteen hundred progeny), not to mention Strom Thurmond . . . In my spiraling existential confusion, I decided that Jennifer and I should make another baby ASAP, and we did. The day we got green-lighted to resume conjugal relations, Grace was conceived. Our Irish-twin girls, now six and five, are insisting they need a baby brother, but so far our Vizsla, Buzz Likeyear, is the best we've been able to come up with.

Because of my half-decent health, hottie wife, and what Richard Ford might call the ultimate good luck, I am not yet in need of Viagra. Even dumb-luckier, fifteen years into our lifelong commitment I'm still head over heels with this girl. Making love with her is how our daughters were conceived, only two of the reasons I sometimes experience far more kinky *and* old-fashioned intimacy in her moist, naked presence than I ever imagined was possible. Yet maybe we've seen each other naked, helped one another to vomit, handled each other's laundry, a few times too often. Neither of our chest-waist-hip ratios is what it used to be—mainly, in Jennifer's case, because she has borne our girls into the world and then nursed them. Cesarean scars may escalate my emotional commitment, but not my libidinal interest.

If you still love and care about your wife but no longer lust, if you ever did, only for her, what are the options? Good Jim is here to tell you that the honorable course is to stay faithful to her, especially if she's the mother of your children. Keep a fifth of *anejo* in the freezer, a spliff in the drawer of your nightstand. Requisition posh lingerie, manufacture scenarios, make catholicguilt.com your home page, augment the mood with accoutrements. Liquor up front, poker in the rear, but avoid any tournaments played in Amsterdam, L.A., or Las Vegas. Hire a babysitter, but only to take care of the kids while you and their mom spend a night at the Hilton. Make do.

What about that old warhorse, honesty? Is it still the best policy, even when admitting to your wife that your desire for her has been reduced by even a single bottom quark, let alone owning up to aspirations that involve other women, would make her feel awful for months? (Or, almost as bad, cause her to wait till you're asleep before stabbing you in the eye with a bowie knife, driving it in all the way up to the hilt, logically enough, in the eye you used to peep at a sunbathing woman, as a jealous wife does in Denis Johnson's "Emergency.") What should you do when you don't have permission to *have* these aspirations, let alone to admit them?

A few years ago a teaching colleague shared with me how he'd "totally unpushily" suggested to his wife that they "might make an interesting threesome" with the unattached red-haired woman living in the riverfront condominium two floors below theirs. The suggestion was greeted with such piercing ululations that he retracted it at once. All I meant was, etc., etc. He and his wife remain undivorced, but they also had to sell their great condo and *move*. As Doyle Brunson might say, she reraised him all-in and he folded.

In poker, extortionate raises are called *coming over the top* of the initial bettor, often abbreviated to, simply, *coming*. To come at most stages of a no-limit tournament involves shoving in *all* of your chips. For one of you then, should your opponent have the nerve to call your huge bet, it's all over. This is a big part of what makes the game so terrifying, ugly, and beautiful. God may play dice with the universe, as Einstein one feared, but serious gamblers, scorning metaphysical crapshoots and the casino's house edge, prefer no-limit Texas hold'em. Light-years removed from the dime-quarter games of kitchen and dorm room, where the most you can lose is your beer money and who walks away with it depends less on skill than on luck, no-limit tournament action is always a ruthlessly disciplined fight to the death. The eros of these contests is evoked by Shana Hiatt's role on World Poker Tour broadcasts, as well as in Web-site names like fulltiltpoker, paradisepoker, and ultimatebet.com, whose ads feature sunbathing babes in bikinis. Because each time you enter a no-limit pot, either online or in a flesh-and-blood tournament, it's an emergency waiting to happen.

Poker players love risk and aggression, and the best are uncannily good at maximizing the monetary value of the hands they've been dealt. When it finally comes down to the highest-order bluffs, money management, and reading ability, the game departs from the realm of science and chance into art. Is poker at this level a reasonable facsimile of truth-telling and legitimate deceit in a marriage? Uh, yup. Do skills developed in one arena enhance your odds of succeeding in the other. Hello? Even so, the most chilling consequences of falsehood and bogus persuasion get multiplied by orders of magnitude when you're talking children and lifelong commitment. Mislead some dude about how big your flush is, lose or win a couple of dimes. Mislead your spouse about where your heart really is, and nothing much good can come out of it; likelier upshots, in my experience, include ICUs, mayhem, dead children. Bottom line? To have as my wife a beautiful woman like Jennifer, who loves me, who is the mother of our daughters and stepmother to Bridget, and who may still want to have another child with me—I cannot risk mucking this up.

No decent husband or father (or poker player) would ever admit this, but getting divorced would also be, well, impractical. No man or woman should underestimate how luxuriously *convenient* it is, as the Church Lady might say, to be married. Even actuaries will attest that both you and your children will live longer, while pollsters say happier, doctors say healthier, your accountant says wealthier. *Stay married or die* says the memo.

Certainly, purchasing big-ticket items together commits you to behaving responsibly over the long haul, or at least for the life of the loan. Credit cards, car payments, tax returns, checking accounts, and thirty-year mortgages all make more sense when you're wed and make being wed make more sense. Take Jennifer and me, for example. People who like to wager on how much they'll earn in the near future versus the value of a house they want *now* can take out an ARM or a jumbo mortgage. We have a Mutumbo. To pay it off, live in the house, enable our daughters to live here, have their own rooms, their own bathroom, walk to school in three minutes, etc., we need to keep our marriage intact. A divorce would just about bankrupt us; worse, it would impoverish our girls. Jennifer lived through a divorce as a child and I lived through one as a parent, so we both know firsthand how devastating it would be to them emotionally. Yet while Jennifer seems to accept this down deep in her cell structure, a few of the algorithms of my DNA's helices insist that I fuck other women. It's not really me, it's my helices. But since I wouldn't want my daughters' husbands' helices to say the things mine do, cosmic justice dictates that Bad Jim go into retirement. Good Jim wants to stay married to Jennifer, to raise our daughters with her, to let them grow up without psychiatrists and antidepressants and custody battles, to see them off to college together and, eventually, to help them raise their own sets of kids.

At my age, though, that isn't likely. It was only two or three years ago that Bea and Grace exited the diaper stage, and the joke around our house is, it won't be that long before it's Daddy's turn again—incentive enough to behave myself. As Jennifer every so often reminds me, "Till death, or Depends, do us part."

In the meantime, Goody Two-Shoes still struggles on occasion with the requisites of marriage and fatherhood. Last fall, for example, on Dads Day at Grace's preschool, Jennifer was forced to do the honors. After summarizing the curriculum, the teacher asked each girl and boy to say in whose lap they were sitting, what his job was, and so on. Eventually Grace was asked where her dad was. In her usual drama-queen fashion, she folded her arms across her chest, unfolded them, put her hands on her hips, got slightly red in the face, and huffed, "He's playing poker. He's *always* playing poker!"

Not true! As a matter of fact, I was off that day supporting my family by making a hoity-toity presentation at Yale University. No less an eminence than Steven Smith, the Alfred Coles Professor of Government, had invited me to talk about literature at a Master's Tea at Branford College—the literature of poker, but still. That eighty people crowded into the Branford reception room was due not at all to my eloquence, anticipated or actual, but to the dozen-plus hold'em games in full swing throughout Yale. I should also admit that I'd asked Professor Smith to schedule my tea to sync up with the World Poker Finals taking place at Foxwoods, about fifty miles northeast of New Haven. Cranking *Love and Theft* and *World Without Tears* but without really pushing my rented yellow Mustang convertible, I made the trip in forty minutes, plunked down my Tea honorarium in a feeder tournament, and five hours later had a $10,200 seat in the championship event. In this sense, I guess, Grace was right.

As far as poker trips to Vegas are concerned, Grace's mom has a small problem with the concept of *what happens here, stays here,* especially after the city's mayor, Oscar Goodman, summed up the situation: "The new brand we're creating is one of freedom based on sensuality." He's also floated the idea that legal bordellos "be used as a redevelopment tool" for downtown by turning a stretch of Fremont Street into "a little Amsterdam." Bad Jim, who travels the poker circuit alone, finds this new brand of urban renewal utterly convincing, whereas Jennifer's take roughly parallels that of Marge Simpson: "Homer! If I'd known there were loose women in Las Vegas, I would never have let you go!"

And besides. The less time I may have with Beatrice and Grace down the road, the more I need to be home with them now. Ditto for Bridget and Jennifer. When I'm not off somewhere playing poker, I can toast bears at tea parties, play catch, help the girls learn to read, even sip cocktails with their mother while attending full-dress reenactments of *Cinderella,* and maybe make love to her afterward. What I can't do, whether I'm home or out of town, is guarantee that things will work out.

Guarantee? Right. That's a good one.

I was home, for example, on Friday the thirteenth of February when Grace was accidentally slashed in the right eye by a two-pronged wire sticking out from the end of a so-called magic wand at a gala children's birthday party a few blocks away. Blood and some blue from her iris began leaking from the two deep lacerations in her cornea. Ninety minutes and three emergency referrals later, we delivered her into the hands of Peter Rabiah, a seasoned, exquisitely talented pediatric ophthalmological surgeon. Dark, slightly balding, visibly tired at the end of a long day and week, Dr. Rabiah determined that Grace had zero vision in the eye, which was shaped like an underinflated basketball someone had stepped on. He needed to put Grace under general anesthesia to try to repair it.

We gaped at him, begging for promises, answers, predictions. He was not optimistic. "This is a serious open-globe injury," he told us in a not-quite-neutral tone of voice. "The visual prognosis is guarded." He also had no choice but to hold my own eye for a few extra beats: "You need to be aware that children this age can die under general anesthesia."

Fear? Love? Commitment? Mind-bending terror? We were wallowing in it, altogether helpless in this good doctor's hands, though endlessly lucky to be there. If we'd arrived at his office fifteen or twenty minutes later, he might have been in a restaurant starting his weekend with a vodka martini, effectively shunting Grace's blind eye under the knife of a junior associate.

Cut to the removal by Dr. Rabiah of the stitches forty-six days later. Post-op exams had predicted this, but now we have the results: the ocular pressure in both eyes is normal; both eyeballs round, firm, and normal. Grace has 20/20 vision in the right eye, 20/15 in the left (because of all the extra work it's been doing). Jennifer and I are grinning like a couple of morons as our eyes start to water and sting. Peter Rabiah is officially and forever The Man. The more enthusiastically we communicate this to him, the more embarrassed he becomes, which just makes him more of The Man. Our gratitude is so overwhelming that, once he leaves the room, Jennifer suggests to me that she "would do anything for the guy," up to and including "you know . . ."

Say what? In the fifteen years I've known her, this is the first time she's gone here, at least in a way that didn't make it clear she was kidding.

"He doesn't wear a ring," she points out.

"Which is relevant how?"

"I just thought . . ."

Yes? Yes? My God! Is she serious? "What about a case of Cristal?" I ask finally.

"Yeah, that too."

She's giddy. I'm giddy. Rabiah's still out of earshot, we hope. We're taking turns hugging our daughter. Like every red-blooded wife, Jennifer has a short list of mostly tall men she has a theoretical dispensation to spend one, but only one, night with: Michael Jordan, Bruce Springsteen, Tom Hanks, Barack Obama, David Letterman. The usual suspects for women her age, all the more unthreatening to me because of their remoteness. As George H. W. Bush would nasally drawl, "Nah gah happen." Dr. Rabiah's different. He couldn't really be much more present, and it's apparently relevant that he seems to be straight and unmarried. And talk about status in Jennifer's eyes! The guy single-handedly restored our baby's vision. Grace's clear, huge, long-lashed, and flashing blue eye had been damaged, perhaps beyond repair; he repaired it. Our insurance will cover all but $200 of the $86,071 bill, but clearly we owe Peter Rabiah much more than money. Don't we owe him at least a Jenny Special? Much to my nervous astonishment, the idea doesn't seem *that* preposterous.

That was six weeks ago. Grace's eye has never worked or looked better, and everyone's eternally grateful. But so—did it happen? Preposterous is as preposterous does, if you know what I'm saying. Has my frisky comedienne repaid her knight in shining armor the most generous way she knows how? Between the half dozen office visits, all the time I have spent out of town on my book tour and or playing tournaments, and the fact that "Peter" lives only three towns away, she certainly *could* have. I would think that I'd know if it happened, but even then I could never be certain. And which would be worse: not knowing it happened, or believing it did when it didn't?

As Yogi Berra reminds us, you can observe a lot of things just by watching. I'm home for another eleven days before heading to Vegas for the final two weeks of the World Series of Poker, and I'd like to find out before then. So after our daughters are safely tucked in, I deploy four and a half decades of poker experience by watching their mom's green Mesopotamian eyes as I ever so casually ask, "How're things with our pal Dr. Rabiah?"

Pregnant pause, during which I remind myself that Penelope waited to tell Odysseus of "all she'd borne at home" until after he slaughtered the suitors, identified the provenance of their bed, and got himself cleaned up and settled in for the evening. Only then does *he* admit to Circe's "deceits and magic," though not to subduing that kinky enchantress in the biblical sense. All he tells his wife of Calypso is that the golden-haired, eternally youthful nymph(o) with an island-size dungeon "detained him there"—for seven years!—"but he held out against her," which while the *case* ain't exactly the truth. The superfine Phaeacian princess Nausicaa, before whom Odysseus appeared on the beach *buck naked,* just doesn't come up in the marriage bed at Ithaca; nor do his camp wives at Troy. What Odysseus tells Penelope is the version of his road trip he knows she wants to hear, which is why they lived happily ever after, at least until Dante caught up with them. Penelope's version of events at home is that, with eligible suitors galore and her husband presumably dead, she remained *aglaopistos* (Homeric Greek for "110 percent committed") to her wily husband every last minute of his twenty-year swath across Mediterranean womanhood.

Jennifer's version is a grin and a shrug, then a wink. I smile, try to smile, but I'm bluffing. Following Rabiah's instructions, she has nursed Grace's eye back to life—filling prescriptions and keeping them straight during three different schedules of drops, making every appointment, implementing restrictions for play dates, making sure Grace didn't fall and bump her head, keeping the aluminum eye shield clean and in place without taping her bangs to her forehead . . . Yeah, but what else did she do? I feel rage and abject curiosity, stupendously lucky and grateful, but I give her my steeliest poker face. *And?* She stretches and yawns, looking comely as hell, but I still don't have clue number one about what to say, what to do, as she moseys down the hall toward our bedroom.

How My Son Got His Name

RICH COHEN

When my son was born, I was wearing the same T-shirt I had been wearing twelve years earlier, when, as a college student in New Orleans, I drank thirteen shots, made public my plan to conquer the world, vomited, and blacked out on the levee. That I was wearing the same T-shirt came to me in a flash. I was rushing the boy—our brand-new addition—out of the delivery room, my wife receding into the distance, fading like a butte in an old western, towards the ICU (the nurse said he wasn't crying right, or breathing right, or something), which, terribly, stands for "intensive care unit" and is filled with skinny, emaciated little baby bodies hooked to tubes and pipes and drains and sucking machines, and the nurses sit around as if it were no big deal doing their nails and reading fashion magazines.

As I went through the lobby, with the boy in his incubator, with the boy on wheels, like a go-cart or a soap box derby racer, and he had eyes, of course, and was looking around, and so my two eyes had now, in a sense, become four eyes, all these people, many of them Hasidic Jews, were standing around, waiting for the elevator. They turned around and looked at me and my son, who, at this point, had no name. He was not called anything and so was pure potential, as unnamed as the animals before the appearance of Adam. For the Hasidim, it must really have been something to see— this father and his brand-new son, these wayward, godless Jews, freaked-out and tearing up the linoleum. When they looked at me, I looked right back. That's something my father taught me. When the Hasidim stare at you, or whenever anyone catches you with the hard look in a weak moment, hold the tears inside your ducts and stare right back. When I did, I caught my reflection, dull but recognizable in the big metal doors of the elevator. I looked beat to hell, wiped out and terribly ugly, but still me—that's when I noticed the T-shirt. I had bought that T-shirt at the Camellia Grill, the great lunch counter at the top of St. Charles Avenue, a boulevard of Victorian mansions and Spanish moss that cuts right through the crescent city. It's a white T-shirt, with the name of the restaurant beneath a big beautiful camellia, pink but fading after years and years of being run through the wash, stretched to fit my expanding postcollege body, comfortable and evocative, and really one of my favorites.

In that hallway of Hasidim, with the tremendous size of the event just hitting me, that pink camellia gave me something to hang on to. It was like a magic ball in which I could glimpse myself at all ages and in all weathers and in all seasons: sitting at the Camellia Grill on a muggy afternoon in August, with a burger and a vanilla shake, trying to kill a hangover, or stoned out of my mind on a Wednesday in the late eighties, or surrounded by friends, ordering the Cannibal, a raw hamburger served on a bun, or sitting at the counter the morning after Jessica and I were engaged—we ate oysters Rockefeller at Antoine's, drank Hurricanes at Pat O'Brian's, drank Sazeracs at the Napoléon House—ordering omelets, which I had long told her were the best omelets and probably the best food in the world. After her third bite, she said, "I always thought there was a lot of exaggeration and fantasy in what you say, but I can now see that everything you say is absolutely true."

This T-shirt, reflected in the elevator doors, was like a device in a movie, a talisman that follows the protagonist through his life like the memory of a lost love, or a lost sled, thus setting everything in perspective. Of course, one of the big lessons of becoming a father (unless you are a special kind of jerk) is that you no longer see yourself as the sole protagonist of your movie: you are now just one of the cast—Mike Brady or Dr. Huxtable—part of the ensemble, and so less likely to win for best actor, but still eligible for best supporting actor, which is not too shabby.

In the seventh month of pregnancy, Jessica and I attended one of those classes where they teach you how to have a baby, how to count and how to breath and how to regard all this counting and breathing. At the beginning of the first class, we had to go around the room and, in the manner of Alcoholics Anonymous, each give our name and say something about ourselves. I went first. I was tentative and embarrassed. I said, "Hello, my name is Richard and my wife, Jessica, is having a baby." This was on the Upper West Side of Manhattan, so, when I said this—"My wife, Jessica, is having a baby"—a whole crowd of pregnant women jumped all over me and, in voices that sang of Westchester and Long Island, shouted, "You're *both* having the baby!"

After me came a Russian guy, who, in callous disregard of the code, which is maybe why the Russians lost the Cold War, decided to make points on my suffering; his answer also demonstrated a sort of comic miscalculation, maybe another reason the Soviet imperium collapsed.

He said, "My name is Demetrius. And I am having baby!"

The teacher, joking, said, "How much weight have you gained, Demetrius?"

And poor Demetrius, all alone now in the blue said, "What? I am fat? You are the one who should be asking yourself about how much weight."

For the rest of class, I sat around listening to tales of breech births and exploding placentas, and staring at some really dirty pictures, and watching the sort of film I had not seen since sex education class in the fifth grade, taught by Mr. Ermis, who drove around in a

VW bus and was called, by me and my friends, "Mr. Spermis." The movie was a lot like that movie *Rudy,* wherein the determined young go-getter will not quit until he fulfills his dream by playing in a football game for Notre Dame, only in this case it's a dogged sperm swimming upstream, through a hidden network of tubes and pipes and black stuff.

But here is what they don't tell you in class: having a baby changes your marriage; having a baby changes *everything*. It makes you see yourself as part of the larger project. It takes you into that section in the Bible dominated by *begats*. It brings a clock into your house and sets that clock running. It gives time a face, and that face sits on your baby as the clouds sit on the sea. It makes the future real. It makes your mind race ahead, far ahead, into the middle of the century, when you will be dead. It makes you know for certain that you are going to die. It makes you acutely aware of the accomplishments and shortcomings of your own parents. It makes you dread the day the boy will turn on you. It makes you understand that life is ninety percent about shit. It takes the great relationship you have forged with your wife—two young people running around, running wild, going on trips, eating in good restaurants, flying for no good reason to New Orleans, having excellent sex—and changes it completely. It makes clear that a lot of things you once suspected were unimportant, but worried about anyway, really are unimportant, so you worry about them still but much less. Because there are other and better things to worry about. Because what is that red mark on the boy's shoulder? What a cute shoulder it is! It puts a booster on the rocket and gives all that energy a direction. *We're going to Mars, boys! They say they've got excellent public schools up there!* When a relationship is based only on the good sex and the good restaurants and the trips to New Orleans, becoming a parent can wreck a marriage—the little boy comes out swinging a hammer. For me, I think—because it is early in the day and I don't want to call down the god of the jinx (I feel the

Hasidim shaking their heads, saying, "Schmuck, there is no god but God")—the boy has come as fulfillment of all those dinners and trips to New Orleans and sex; that part is biology, of course, and so goes without saying.

That is, you say the vows in front of Rabbi Bronstein, and when you get choked up, he says, *Alright, Let it all out, let it all out,* and you walk away with a grand Hollywood sense of promise and commitment, and yet, when the boy is born, that first sense of commitment doubles and doubles and doubles again. You turn from two people who love each other into a team, a pair forever linked in the imagination of another person—the boy. In his mind, you are one person, so, in a sense, that is what you are obligated to try to become. You fuse like words, like melon and water. You become the ma and pa of primal imagination.

That's why some people freak on the whole idea of parenthood. It is why some new fathers start lifting weights or driving a Harley, while others turn into superparents and fill their houses with mind-twisting puzzles and classical music they probably hate—music they once regarded as little more than a sad background for Christmas trips to the mall. This idea of living in the mind and imagination of someone else can be pretty hard to take. It is one of the many times in life that you are defined by your circumstance—the new kid, the Jew kid, the dumb kid, the kid in back, the rookie, the pledge, the virgin, the slut, the young parent.

It is why, in the park, when people see that you are part of a couple that is pregnant—or, as a guy I know said, "We're preggers, dude"—they feel the need to ask a million questions and say how great it is and then tell you that in fact it's terrible and hard and you will never sleep again or see a movie or eat out or enjoy the kind of sex I call *sweet sweet love.* I suppose it's their way of telling you who they are: what they went through, what they survived. In such cases, you have to fight hard to define yourself, and not be defined. Not a father, or a guy with a two-month-old, or a guy without sleep. You have to say, I am still me and Jessica is still Jessica, only now there is one more and so we are bigger and stronger. Or as the God of Genesis says, Go forth and procreate. Which means, Go forth and *fuck, fuck, fuck*. When God promised to scatter the seed of Abraham like stars in the skies, he might have been promising a big family and a grand legacy, or he might have been promising lots of great and various sex.

Of course, in the pregnant months, all this lies in the future. In those months, you become a welcoming committee, a homecoming committee, planning a party, ordering streamers and painting walls and coming up with a clever yet not too threatening theme. Was this all clear to me when Jessica first came out of the bathroom and said the line had turned blue? I am sure not. The first real sense of it came when we were at the doctor's office for the sonogram, and they ran that wand across her belly, and the screen came to life. The graphics sucked. There was no color, no action, no fight scenes, no explosions, no characters—well, there was one character. I will call him Blinky. It was the first image of a heartbeat, the debut of the great hammering motor that will power the boy, God willing, into the next century. It seemed to be coming not from in here but from out there, from deep space—we were staring into a radio telescope and that blip was an alien craft that had been picked up on the edge of the solar system, passing through the orbit of Pluto, say, barreling toward Earth—it would arrive in approximately nine months; it would touch down at Lennox Hill Hospital in Manhattan. This baby would be a visitor from another planet, a soul sent down into a body, that bumbles and jabbers and shits her pants because all of this is new and a rookie has to learn to operate the space suit and move through the atmosphere before he can stand and stare at the sky and wonder, "Where the fuck am I?"

When the boy was born, the nurse cleaned him off and stood him up and carried him across the room. She blew him dry as if he were a car that had just come through the wash. He reached out and

110

stretched and seemed cool and sharp. He did not cry. Not for a moment. He just looked at me. And I looked back. And the nurse pounded on him frantically, saying, "I want to hear a cry. I want to hear one good cry!" When she did not hear that one good cry, she loaded him into an incubator and told me to push the boy and follow her to the ICU for testing. Then we were passing through all those Hasidim, a tunnel of beards and eyes. I looked at the Hasidim and looked at the boy and a name popped into my head: Isaac. As if it came from God. As if Yahweh himself were in my head saying, "And you shall call him Isaac."

When I came back to the room, and it felt crummy coming back alone, though it was one of the last times Jessica and I would ever be alone together, and we waited for the results of the tests—he was fine, not a ding in the fender, so maybe I was not projecting; maybe he really was too cool for this world, or for that nurse anyway—I told her about my experience, and how it was almost mystical, and how all those Hasidim were staring at me, and how we should call the boy Isaac. She frowned. I had to admit that Isaac was a pretty crappy name. I could only think of the bartender on *Love Boat,* or of this counselor at my childhood camp named Isaac whom I was warned to stay away from: he always wanted to give me a back rub. So I thought, maybe that was not the voice of God after all. Maybe it was just my own voice. Maybe I had seen those Hasidim, then, because he was a Hasid, I thought of the great writer Isaac Bashevis Singer, and that's where the name came from. The more I thought of this, the more right it felt, so, in the end, God, Jessica, and I came up with a compromise: Aaron. Aaron Bogart Cohen. Which is still super-Jewy and Old Testament–y and also had the great advantage of being the name of the New York Yankee who, a few days before, had beaten the Boston Red Sox with a dramatic late-game home run in Yankee Stadium: here I am thinking of Aaron Boone. Besides, God would not be raising the boy. Jessica and I would be raising the boy, so Jessica and I should choose the name.

111

Then Aaron was out of ICU, and my brother-in-law picked us up in his big fancy car and the three of us went home—the new family, the new promise, the new commitment, the new adventure. And that of course is when the real shit started. It's like a lot of things: you make it happen, then it happens to you.

The Wedding of the Century

JOHN SEABROOK

When I was very young, I listened to the story of how my parents met as if it were the story of the creation. I suppose it was, in a way, the story of my creation, but that isn't what I found so enthralling. Hearing my mother tell it, watching the sapphire in her engagement ring sparkle as she gestured, and seeing my father, if he was around (he wasn't very often), or listening (he usually perked up for the parts about himself), lower the flap of his newspaper and interject a comment—the story transformed what was just a coincidence into something that felt like destiny. I believed in the romance of the story and think I believed that a marriage could never go wrong as long as the story came out right.

Later, when I was old enough to imagine marrying, I assumed I would meet my wife under equally romantic circumstances. Later still, when I did meet her (she was the copy editor on a piece I wrote about Dan Quayle—not exactly the stuff of fairy tales), I tried to use what I knew of my parents' meeting and courtship as a guide in my own blind leap into marriage. But their story kept leading me astray, and finally I had to forget about it and find my own way.

Now I've been married for twelve years, and maybe I'm ready to tell the story myself, putting in what they told me and imagining some things that might have been left out, hoping it will still come out right in the end.

It begins, as it always began, on a crisp but springlike day—April

4, 1956. The SS *Constitution*, an ocean liner, is waiting at Pier 84 in New York City, ready to carry Grace Kelly and her family, along with fifty-five friends and a small press contingent, to "The Wedding of the Century" in Monaco. Among the ticketed passengers are my parents, although they haven't yet met. My father is one of the wedding guests, and my mother is a reporter, covering the wedding for the United Press, later rechristened the United Press International. They're waiting for fate, in the form of a ship, to carry them down the Hudson River and into the ocean of possible destinies.

But the deck was still crowded with unticketed visitors who had to go ashore before the ship could leave. Some were society people, raising glasses in one last toast to the glorious twenty-six-year-old bride, "Gracie" to her friends, who wore dark glasses, a pale yellow scarf on her flyaway hair, and was holding her white French poodle, Oliver, in her arms. There were dozens of journalists who had not been lucky enough to secure tickets on board and were hoping for a photo or an item to run in the evening papers, because ever since the news of the movie star's engagement to the prince had become official, around Christmastime, the public's demand for the story had been insatiable. For the society reporters, used to having their work consigned to the back of the newspaper, the Kelly-Rainier wedding was a chance to bask in the light of the front page. Photographers were leaping from the gangplank to the deck, in spite the ship's officers attempts to stop them. John B. Kelly-Grace's bull-in-a-China-shop father, had already gotten into a scuffle with one photographer. The wedding was becoming something of a circus, which Grace and her family had been hoping to avoid, and they hadn't even left the dock yet.

Standing by the ship's railing, taking notes on the scene, was Elizabeth Toomey, a single, thirty-two-year-old UP staff reporter, who was, along with her colleague Helen Thomas, the best-known female byline on the UP's news service. Her daily column, "Woman's View," ran in the *New York World-Telegram* and dozens of other papers around the country. She had got the taste for real news reporting shortly after graduating from Missouri's Columbia School of Journalism, twelve years earlier, when many of the men who would have been in her class were away at the war and she was given opportunities that a woman wouldn't ordinarily have received. But when the war ended and the men came back, she returned to the women's beat—weddings, food, clothes, and the occasional feature story on an actress. Apart from the occasional interview with Margaret Truman, and the odd exclusive on a troubled starlet, her stories rarely made news.

Just before Christmas, in a run-of-the-mill phone interview with Grace Kelly—her editors had asked for a column on what the stars were expecting from Santa—Liz had brought up a rumor she had heard, but didn't believe, that Grace was planning to marry the prince of Monaco. There's no way that's going to happen, she had argued to the reporter who had passed along the rumor during lunch at the Pen and Pencil, a reporters' hangout on Third Avenue, around the corner from the UP offices on Forty-second Street, because Grace Kelly was an independent, self-reliant, modern American woman, and the princess of Monaco would necessarily be a slave to Old World conventions, a mere adjunct to the prince. Grace Kelly would never even play that role in a movie (although, since Hitchcock's *To Catch a Thief,* starring Grace and Cary Grant, filmed on location in Monaco, was still in the movie theaters, it wasn't hard to imagine Grace in a Mediterranean setting)—to say nothing of real life.

What if they're in love? her colleague asked.

Oh, pooh—love, Liz replied. There had been men who claimed to be in love with her, and she thought she might be in love with one or two of them, but in the end she was glad she had never allowed herself to be tied down.

Well, what if it isn't love? the man went on. What if Grace is marrying him for the money, and he's marrying her for the publicity?

"Grace Kelly has freedom," Liz said with complete conviction. "For a woman, that's harder to come by than love or money."

Still, Liz thought it wouldn't hurt to ask Grace about the rumor, so over the phone she said, "There's talk that you'll be getting an engagement ring for Christmas from Prince Rainier," and waited for Grace to laugh it off. Instead there was a silence on the other end of the phone.

Liz thought the line must have gone dead, so she said, "Hello?"

"I heard you," Grace answered in that famous voice, amused and a trifle coy.

More silence. And then she added, "I can't imagine a nicer gift."

So Liz ran with the story that Grace was planning to marry, and that "Miss Kelly's marriage to the handsome prince probably will signal the end of her highly successful movie career." It was a huge scoop for Elizabeth Toomey, although she was characteristically modest about it, saying it was just luck she'd had the interview scheduled at that time. She figured Grace had favored her because of her Irish name.

Liz was counting on the Kelly wedding to free her from the women's beat. Over the next two weeks, she would have a chance to make front pages all over the world, provided she could come up with the stuff. A big story or two, and she felt she could force her editors to move her onto a more serious topic by threatening to move to another news service if they refused.

But getting a story her colleagues didn't have was going to be difficult. The Kellys had tried to stop reporters from traveling to Monaco with them, and when that failed, they had reserved the first-class deck for themselves and their guests, and confined the press below, to cabin class. The only exception would be dinner— the press were invited up to the first-class dining room—but they had to keep to their own tables and not approach the other guests with questions.

"I'll tell you what you have to do," said Liz's editor before she left. "You'll just have to get one of the single men in the Kelly party to fall for you."

"That is a shocking suggestion," she said with a laugh, "and I'm going try to forget you said it."

But she hadn't forgotten, and as Liz stood by the railing, mentally estimating the size of the crowd, an old habit—dividing by twos until she'd whittled the group down to a number she could count, then multiplying by twos again—she was wondering which of the eligible-looking men might be among her fellow passengers. That was when she first laid eyes on my father.

He was obviously with the Kelly party, because he kept topping off their champagne glasses, using bottles he kept stashed somewhere on deck. He was tall and slick-looking and dressed in a loud, checked sports jacket and obviously full of himself. Liz thought she recognized his face—she prided herself on never forgetting a face—but couldn't remember where she'd seen it.

Finally the deck was cleared. Then the ship's horn sounded with a deafening blast, and there was a thunk and a low vibration as the propellers began to turn. Slowly the ship backed out of its bay, spun, and began to slide down the Hudson River. The passengers remained on deck, watching as the city skyline unspooled before them, until the *Constitution* passed through the Verrazano Narrows—there was no bridge yet—and headed for the open sea.

My mother was sharing a cabin with two other women. One was Jinx Falkenburg, a former World War II pinup girl and actress (she played Sue Dolan in the 1939 film *The Lone Ranger Rides Again*), who by the 1950s had become a radio and television personality; she and her husband, Tex McCrary, were the Regis and Kathie Lee of their day. The other was Cynthia Lowry, from the AP, unmarried and in her early forties. The cabin was full of flowers, all for Jinx, and there were also a lot of leather shoes, bags, and belts, because a leather manufacturer was one of Jinx's sponsors. Jinx wasn't in the room yet, and Liz said to Cynthia that they had to be firm and not let her have any more closet space than they had. But when Jinx turned up, she was so charming that they changed their minds.

Because the press was dining in first class, they would be required to dress for dinner, and that meant long dresses for the ladies and black tie for the men. Liz owned one long dress, and she had borrowed two more. She hung them in the closet, wondering if Jinx might let her borrow some of the shoes in the room.

"Say, Jinx?"

"What's that, darling?"

"Did you say you had a list of people in the Kelly party who are aboard the ship?"

"I sure do. You can't tell the players apart without a scorecard."

"Could I take a look at it? I saw someone earlier I thought I recognized, but I could not think of who he was."

Jinx produced the list and Liz looked it over, noting with satisfaction the preponderance of Irish names. John Seabrook was not one of them. Then she remembered where she had seen that face. It was in *Life,* maybe six months earlier, in a big spread about the frozen-food company built by the Seabrooks—a father and his three sons. John Seabrook was one of the sons. He had a persistent PR agent in New York, a man named Lynn Famol, who had tried several times to get Liz to write a story about his client— the Spinach King, as Seabrook had immodestly dubbed himself.

"You girls know a fellow named John Seabrook?"

"Sure," said Jinx. "I've seen him around New York. Jack, I think, is what he calls himself."

"What do you know about him?"

"Not married, if that's what you mean, though I think he used to

118

be. Kind of a ladies man. He had a thing with Eva Gabor, and I think Ann Miller after that. Regular at '21,' and the Stork Club. Good-looking, always wears beautiful clothes, and seems like he must have money, though probably not as much as he looks like he has."

"Why do you say that?"

"He tries a little too hard to look the part. You're interested in him, aren't you?"

"No, I'm not," Liz said truthfully. She was only thinking that if she didn't get any interviews with European royalty, she might have to settle for a Spinach King.

It was a long-standing custom of the now vanished culture of transatlantic crossings that passengers were not required to dress for dinner on the first night out, to allow them time to unpack and get their things in order. Jack Seabrook had learned this bit of worldly wisdom from his father. During the 1920s, his father was often overseas, where his engineering company had a number of road- and dock-building projects, and on the few occasions when he returned, he would regale his family with stories of who was on the ship and exactly what they wore, ate, drank, and talked about. Shipboard was an excellent place to study the habits of the leisured class, because there was inevitably more interplay between the different social strata than on dry land. Jack's father was not an educated man, but he was intelligent and had a keen eye, and he would often say he learned everything he needed to know about how to pass himself off as cultured and well-to-do by observing the wealthy passengers on these ocean crossings. He imparted this knowledge to his son, which was one reason Jack was more or less at ease among the Kelly party, even though most of them had more distinguished pedigrees than he had.

Jack had a private cabin, which was fortunate, because except for his bed all the space was filled with clothes and cases of champagne.

He had appointed himself unofficial sommelier for the crossing and put the word out among the guests that if they wanted to drink good champagne, he was the man to see. He liked being an authority. He was thirty-nine and knew Grace through her father, John B., whose construction firm had built the main factory for Seabrook Farms. He didn't know Grace as well as he knew Peggy, Grace's older sister, who was more of a Philadelphia party girl. After Jack's first marriage had ended, around the time he was thirty, he'd played the field in Philadelphia and dated some of Peggy's friends, but was never serious about any of them. In recent years, he'd taken over a number of business responsibilities from his father, who was in poor health, and he had begun to think of marrying again and spending more time on the farm. But he wasn't going to repeat the mistake of his first marriage and choose a woman who would find the country life dull.

Grace's guests were required to pay for their own passage and accommodation in Monte Carlo. Jack hoped to offset the expense, and then some, with the publicity he would receive as a wedding guest. Seabrook Farms couldn't hope to match the advertising budgets of their competitors, Birds Eye and General Foods, and so they relied on free publicity as much as possible. In those days frozen foods were advertised as luxury items—products for the sophisticated modern woman who preferred to spend her evenings in some more exalted and culturally stimulating pursuit than boiling vegetables. Jack made a point of getting his name in the society columns written by Walter Winchell, Cholly Knickerbocker, and Dorothy Kilgallen as often as possible because he thought the women who read those columns would thus be more inclined to buy his frozen peas and spinach than the products of his competitors.

His press agent, Lynn Famol, had made a list of the reporters on the ship, and Jack had studied it and planned to meet as many of them as possible. He noted with satisfaction that most of them were women; he felt he had an advantage with women writers, who were inclined to respond to his charm,.

"I've got a great idea," said Famol when they had spoken in his New York office a few days earlier. "You could plant an item with one of the reporters that her royal highness to be is a big fan of Seabrook Farms frozen vegetables, and that she's planning to introduce Rainier to them in the palace."

"The Princess and the Frozen Pea," Jack replied, laughing.

"I love it!"

Dressed now, Jack strolled into the dining room and spotted three women, all of whom were evidently members of the press. One he recognized as Jinx Falkenburg, but the others were unknown to him. Clearly they didn't know about the first-night rule, because they had got themselves done up in gowns.

"Good evening, ladies," he said, making a little bow. "Jinx, how are you?"

"I'm overdressed," she said with a laugh. "How are you, Jack? You're looking debonair as always. Do you know my friends Cynthia Lowry and Liz Toomey?"

"Nice to see you," he said, just in case he'd actually met them before. But he'd have remembered having met this one, he thought to himself, shaking hands with my mother.

"Elizabeth Toomey, United Press," she said, and she raised her jaw a little, as though challenging him to disprove it. "Your press man has been saying I should meet you. Wants me to do a story on the miracle of frozen food, releasing the woman from the bondage of housewifery, so that she can enjoy the bondage of marriage more completely."

"It doesn't sounds like you're convinced," said Jack, amused.

"Instant coffee is about as domestic as I get. What I need is some sort of frozen-food version of my column—just pop a couple of notes in boiling water and presto, six hundred words."

Jinx and Cynthia had drifted away to their table but Liz lingered.

"So," Jack said, "are you having a good crossing so far?"

"I guess it's good," Liz said. "It's my first. We don't have oceans in Missouri." She pronounced it "Missour-a" as people did back in St. Louis.

"Well, it's calm," said Jack. "The sea is, anyway."

"And the bride?"

"The bride is—but I'm not supposed to tell you anything about the bride." The truth is, Jack had seen little of the bride during the round of New York parties that had preceded the *Constitution*'s departure. The nearest he could get was "Kell," her oarsman brother, who only seemed to want to talk about the U.S. rowing team's chances in the upcoming Olympics—a subject my father could not have cared about less.

"Let me ask you something, off the record," Liz ventured. "What do you think of this marriage?"

"What do you mean?"

"I mean doesn't it surprise you that Grace is actually going through with it, even though it means she'll never act in films again?"

"I think Grace is maybe more of a traditional girl than you might think she is. She comes from a big family, and she wants a family of her own, I think, more than anything. And she's a Catholic."

"But she could have a family and a career."

"It isn't as easy as that. Do you have a family?"

"I have a mother. I'd like children, but I don't see how I'd have time for it."

"What if someone like Rainier came along and said, 'Marry me, and you'll never have to work again.' Wouldn't you jump at the chance?"

"Well, in the first place my circle of friends doesn't include too many princes. And in the second place, call me crazy, but, no, I wouldn't jump at the chance to stay home and raise the children and get my husband's dinner on the table every night for the rest of my life." Liz realized this had come out a little more stridently than she had meant it to. So she laughed and said, "But, thanks to the miracle frozen foods, women will have time for careers and the cooking."

One of Jack's Philadelphia friends, Matt McCloskey, came up and said hello. McCloskey was the owner and the publisher of the *Philadelphia Daily News*. Mrs. McCloskey was with him. Jack made the introductions.

"This is Elizabeth Too-may."

"Too-mee," she said.

"Ah, one of the chosen people," said McCloskey, putting on a bit of the Irish. He was a big man with a red face that was always smiling. His wife had on a diamond necklace that looked as if it must be worth a fortune.

"That I be," said Liz, but she always felt a bit funny about playing up her Irish side because she wasn't Catholic. Liz's grandfather, the son of Irish immigrants, had been Catholic but had run away from his religion and his home in Brooklyn around 1870, because, he said, the wicked priests had beaten him in school. He had eventually found his way out to the far edge of the frontier, the Black Hills of South Dakota, which was where Liz was born.

Jack said, "Miss Toomey is covering the wedding for—UP, is it? I'm sure we'll all be reading her over the next two weeks to find out all that we've missed."

"I doubt that," Liz said. "We aren't even allowed up to the first-class deck, where the action is. That is, unless one of you fellows invites me."

"Hang on," said McCloskey as he held up a finger. "I have an idea. Listen, before I left town I got together with my people at the paper and we knocked around the idea of my sending back some columns, you know, dispatches from the crossing and the wedding and so forth. But the thing is—I can't write." He laughed again. "I don't know the first thing about writing. All I know how to write is my name on the checks."

"That's the most important part," said Jack.

"So what I'm thinking now is, Miss Toomey, you could come around with me to some of these silly cocktail parties we have every night, and I'll try to remember what I see when you're not around, and you could cobble it altogether and write a few columns under my byline. How's that sound?"

That sounds like it's exactly what I need, thought Liz. But to McCloskey she said, "I don't know. What about my own stuff—can I also use what I get from you in my UP dispatches?"

"I don't see why not. Just so long as you don't reserve anything you get from me exclusively for yourself."

"Sure, I can live with that. How much per column?"

"The girl doesn't mince words," said Jack.

"Oh, I don't know. What do you think I should pay her, Jack?"

"We don't want to spoil her."

"If you get me a hundred dollars, I'll give you ten percent," said Liz to Jack.

"A hundred it is then," said McCloskey, and he shook hands with my mother.

"And I will waive my fee if you'll agree to meet me after dinner for a drink," said my father.

"Deal," said Liz, thinking that one hundred dollars was a lot more than UP paid her for a column.

The press were all seated together at a table, and their group seemed to make more noise and have more fun than the other tables. Midway through dinner, a magnum of champagne arrived, with a card from Jack Seabrook, written in French. He didn't speak a word of French; the waiter had written it out for him. *À la belle écrivaine, Elizabeth Toomey.* The other reporters were delighted.

"You work fast," said Jinx.

"He's just hoping I'll put him into one of my columns," said my mother out of the corner of her mouth, while giving my father a wave.

"Maybe, but as your older and wiser and lonelier roommate, I'd advise you to be nice to him," said Cynthia. "He's a catch."

"At least be nice enough to keep the champagne coming," said the photographer from *Life*, lifting his glass and nodding in Jack's direction.

Toward the end of dinner a cable came from New York for Liz asking for five hundred words for the morning. So she went down to her room and banged something out on her little portable typewriter, mentioning several of the people on Jinx's list, but not Jack Seabrook—he wasn't going to manipulate her that easily. When she was finished, she took the copy up to the cable operator and waited while he sent it. Then she went to bed. She never gave the after-dinner drink a second thought.

The lifeboat drill was scheduled for the following morning. For the press, it was an opportunity to take photos of the princess to be, in a scarf and dark glasses and sensible shoes, wearing a life vest and listening attentively as the ship's officers explained the procedure. Liz was there, and in a photograph *Life*'s man Howell Conant took of the event, she's standing not far from Grace, smiling at some joke that has just been made, and she's great looking. If you didn't know which one was the movie star, you'd think my mother who was the girl on her way to marry a prince. Which I guess she was, though she didn't know it yet.

Liz felt a tap on her shoulder and saw that it was Jack Seabrook. "I waited for you last night," he said. She looked at him blankly for a moment, then remembered. The drink.

"Oh, I'm sorry, I completely forgot. I had to file after dinner and then I just went straight to bed."

Jack seemed satisfied with this explanation; indeed he seemed rather pleased that she was more interested in her work than in him. In spite of his confident exterior, he was shy, and he felt more relaxed around women who didn't expect him to be charming.

In the afternoon Matt McCloskey sent Liz a message saying that one of the bridesmaids was throwing a cocktail party that evening, which he would be attending with Mrs. McCloskey. If Liz was interested in coming, a steward could fetch her around seven. Liz sent a message back saying that she would be ready.

Almost every evening during the crossing there were two or three cocktail parties aboard the *Constitution*, each hosted by a different guest and generally attended by all the same people. Some were held in the public salons that were scattered around the ship, others in the larger of the private staterooms. *An Affair to Remember,* the 1957 film starring Deborah Kerr and Cary Grant, which is about two strangers who meet and fall in love on a transatlantic crossing, was filmed aboard the SS *Constitution*, and many of the scenes in that film are played out in the same places where my future parents met each other during their crossing.

When Liz entered the McCloskeys' stateroom, she saw Mrs. McCloskey arrayed in even more diamonds than she had been wearing on the previous evening.

"I suppose you're not worried about real life imitating the movies," said Liz. "I mean, some Monaco cat burglar stealing your jewels, as in *To Catch a Thief.*

"Matt and I saw that movie a couple of months ago in Philadelphia," said Mrs. McCloskey, "and to tell the truth, the possibility of a robbery did occur to me. But Matt checked with the hotel and they told him the security would be exceptionally heavy, so we decided to risk it. I mean, if you can't wear your jewelry at a royal wedding, where can you wear it?"

"But just in case," said her husband, "we took out some extra insurance."

Jack was at the party, looking sleek in black tie. He seemed to Liz to be hovering around her, she suspected because he wanted to make sure his name got into print. However, he turned out to be an invaluable source on the other people she saw around the room. He was enough of an insider to be privy to most of the gossip, but enough of an outsider to have studied everyone's background and troubled to remember all the details. He gave Liz the lowdown on the three of Grace's six bridesmaids who were on board. There was Marcee Frisby Pamp, a childhood friend from Philadelphia, who was recently divorced from Mr. Pamp and had brought along an escort. A native Philadelphian, she was Grace's oldest friend among the six, tall and blond and not much given to small talk. There was Bettina Thompson Gray, athletic in a horsey way, and her husband, Frank, a balding, somewhat plump Boston blue blood who worked in banking. And there was Judy Balaban Kanter, whose husband, Jay Kanter, was Grace's agent, and whose father, Barney Balaban, was the head of Paramount Studios. Only twenty-three, but already married for three years, she was the youngest of the bridesmaids.

Jack also pointed out Margaret Kelly, Grace's mother; John B., the father; Kell; and Peggy, who was Grace's older sister, slim and blond and the life of every party, always laughing, a cigarette in her hand, standing near her then husband, George "Gabby" David, and their two daughters. Lizanne, Grace's younger sister, would not be attending the wedding because she was seven months pregnant.

And there was Grace, in a slate blue organza evening dress, carrying a white mink stole. She generally attended the parties only long enough to greet the hosts and make sure everyone was having a good time.

"Do you want to meet the bride?" Jack asked.

"I suppose I should, though I'm not sure if she's going to be too pleased to find me here."

"I'll just say you're doing a story on me, and getting a little background on my friends."

127

"All right, but don't mention that I was the one who broke the news of the wedding. Hopefully she won't remember my name."

They moved in Grace's direction, and when there was a pause, Jack said, "Grace, there's someone I'd like you to meet—Elizabeth Toomey."

Grace's blue-gray eyes turned steely. "I know who you are. You're the one who can't keep a secret."

"I'm sorry if that displeased you, but I thought it was what you wanted."

Grace smiled grudgingly and said, "Watch out for this one, Jack." Then she moved on.

"She's a big fan of our frozen peas, you know," Jack said, watching her go.

"Is that so?"

"I hear she's planning to serve them in the palace."

"Who'd you get that from, your press agent?"

"Why—yes, as a matter of fact. How did you know?"

"It's got that ring to it. Maybe you should try it out on Winchell."

Watching her move around the room, Liz had the impression that Grace too was a guest at her own wedding—that in spite of her self-possession she wasn't in control at all. The wedding belonged to the world now—Liz herself had had something to do with that—and events were going forward as steadily and relentlessly as the SS *Constitution*. Grace seemed almost scared—you could see it most of all in her walk, which looked tentative and unsure.

Liz mentioned these impressions to Jack, and he agreed with her. "You know, in spite of having millions of fans, Grace has never really had anyone on her side," he said, "except perhaps her agent over there, and that's just a commercial relationship. Even her father, though he is certainly proud to be here, has never really supported her, not the way he dotes on Peggy. He always says he can never understand how Grace got to be the movie star, when Peggy's the one with all the talent."

These words touched Liz, not only because they seemed insightful and showed a sensitivity in Jack she had not felt before, but also because she had never had anyone on her side either. Her father had died when she was nine, and her mother had devoted most of her energy to her older sister, Isabel, who was supposedly the talented one—and indeed Isabel could sing and play the piano wonderfully well. But Isabel had also inherited the family weakness for alcohol and by 1956 was already well started on making a mess out of her life. Liz, who sent her mother part of her paycheck each month, would soon be taking care of Isabel too. She never complained about any of this, because she had never expected anything else from life. She'd given up on the prospect of having a family of her own long ago; she had contracted scarlet fever when she was a child, and her mother always told her she should never have children because her weakened heart wouldn't stand the strain. But now, watching Grace leave the room, she allowed herself to wonder, just for a moment, what *would* it be like to have someone take care of you?

Nineteen fifty-six was a year of crisis and growing darkness in the world. The Hungarian revolution, which succeeded briefly in the spring of that year, would be crushed by Stalin in the fall. The hydrogen bomb had been tested above Bikini atoll in May, and the Suez Crisis, triggered by Nasser in July, began the modern cycle of violence in the Middle East. The three main sources of fear in the world for decades to come, the Cold War, nuclear proliferation, and the Arab-Israeli conflict, were all in place by the end of the year. Ten years earlier, it had been possible for people of my parents' generation to believe that in defeating the Nazis they had made the world a safer place. But by the end of 1956, that belief seemed impossibly naïve.

Which is partly why the wedding of the century, coming in the middle of this pivotal year, was such a newsworthy event. In affirming the institution of marriage, and the traditional roles of men and woman in marriage, Grace and the prince offered people a reason to believe that the world wasn't changing so much after all. It was still a woman's job to be a wife—to provide her husband with a home, food, sex, and children. The man worked for the money to buy the house, the car, the jewelry, the children's educations. Just as events were pushing the world toward a frightening, unknown future, the SS *Constitution* was steaming back through time to a predictable, comfortable past.

In later years my father would maintain he knew he wanted to marry my mother from the first time he saw her. I think that he was simply ready to get married again. He had learned his lesson, the first time around, and as he often told me, that lesson was "monogamy." (He always pronounced it as though no one had ever sounded the word before—*mon-o-ga-my*.) I have always had the impression that whereas my father's first marriage was an affair of passion and youth, his second marriage, to my mother, was a more calculated decision to make a match that he thought would last. He was right, and I'm grateful for that, because failed marriages seem to run in families—one of the strongest parts of my marriage comes from the knowledge that both sets of our parents stayed married. But I also think he put some other part of himself away, in deciding to marry again, and in doing so denied my mother a passion she might have found with someone else. She could have asked for more, but then she always asked for so little—she was just the baby sister who was happy with whatever came her way.

It's not as though my father were incapable of passion. Once, when I was ten or eleven years old, I found a shoebox full of old letters tucked away in a dusty corner of the basement in the house where I grew up. They were letters between my father and his first wife—not only her letters, but his too; she must have returned them to him at some point during or after their divorce. Her letters were chatty and affectionate, but his, mainly written when he was still a teenager (he married when he was twenty-one), were full of embarrassingly gushy endearments—the letters of an unworldly boy to the first girl he had ever loved. I was stunned, reading them, because I had never heard my father use language remotely like this with anyone in our family. Maybe he never felt that way again about anyone, after his first marriage ended.

The rest of the trip passed uneventfully. Grace was seen less and less; she was said to be trying to cram in as much French as possible, so she could get through the ceremony without discrediting herself in front of her new subjects.

Liz was the toast of her editors in New York for the stream of dazzling anecdotes she cabled, for morning, afternoon, and evening editions, with the dateline "Aboard the SS *Constitution*, at sea." She wrote about Grace's shuffleboard contests with her sister Peggy, and her all-night charades game—"she kicked off her heels and frantically acted out an advertising slogan, 'Watch the Danger Zone,' but her team failed to guess it and she lost." She reported Grace was practicing making loops in her signature so that it would be more regal, and that the only man she would fox-trot with was her father. One day, "Miss Kelly wept when a passing ship, the SS *Independence*, saluted her with its earsplitting whistles that spelled out 'G-L-G' in Morse code—'Good Luck Grace.'"

In the evenings, my father kept sending champagne to the table, and Jinx and Cynthia kept imploring my mother to pay him more attention. Perhaps my mother sensed that her indifference was what kept my father interested—had she actually made a play for him, like a lot of other women he met, she might have scared him off. Or perhaps, as she always said, she was too busy with the story to think about Jack Seabrook. They did dance in the evening a number of times, not very successfully; somehow their knees kept banging together. ("It was the rolling of the ship!" my father would always

131

interject at this point in the story.) Also, he was inclined to sing along with his favorite songs like "Arrivederci, Roma," which didn't help their timing.

Jack asked several times if she was truly committed to working for the rest of her life, and Liz admitted that she was a bit tired of always having to worry about paying the rent and supporting her mother, and it might be nice to have a break from that and maybe try to have a family—though she'd like to have one more really glorious scoop before she put away her notebook.

The final night, there was an extended round of toast making, and my father made an eloquent one. He was always a gifted after-dinner speaker—he seemed more comfortable talking in public than tête-à-tête. He said, "I think we lucky few who were privileged to be on board this ship will mark these eight days as a turning point in our own lives, and remember this crossing as a passage into a country that we had heard tell of, but didn't know for certain existed, until now—the country of true love."

Jinx kicked Liz under the table when she heard that. But actually, Liz didn't need any prodding. "It was the most romantic thing I'd ever heard anyone say."

On the morning of April 12, the *Constitution* appeared in the harbor at Monte Carlo, and the prince came out to fetch Grace on the royal yacht, *Deo Juvante II*, which he planned to give her as a wedding present. Grace, carrying Oliver, wore an enormous apricot-colored hat and dark glasses, which the press hated, because no one could see her face. As Elizabeth Tommey faithfully reported, the couple did not kiss. "Rainier strode out to the gangplank to help her aboard, and he reached out his arms as if to kiss her. But Oliver the poodle apparently came between them and the prince instead gave Grace something like an awkward handshake."

The passengers disembarked and were taken to one of two hotels, the Hôtel de Paris and the Hermitage. The Kellys stayed in the palace, from which the press was excluded.

The UP had rented a croupier's apartment to use as their head-quarters. It was a railroad flat, and the bedroom window had a view over the palace wall and into the grounds. In addition to my mother, the UP had a cable operator and a bilingual secretary to work the phones. But there wasn't much for any of them to do. The Kelly family had been mostly tolerant of the press, but the Rainiers were a different story. Having reluctantly agreed to let MGM film the wedding—that was the studio's condition for letting Grace out of her contact—Rainier and his family felt they had fulfilled their obligation to the public and arranged virtually no events for the press. Matt McCloskey told Liz that they couldn't continue their collaboration; Grace had put the kibosh on it. Her string of brilliant dispatches abruptly dried up. With the wedding still another week away, the press had resorted to interviewing one another. Jack didn't have much more news than Liz did, but he was happy to tell her whatever he knew.

On Thursday, five days after their arrival in Monaco, they were having drinks in the bar at the Hotel de Paris when Matt McClos-key appeared. He was in a hurry and seemed a bit flustered. He said he needed to speak to my father, in private. They got up and went out to the lobby, and in a few minutes my father returned to the table.

"Something's happened," he said.

"What is it?"

"I'm not supposed to tell you."

"But you will tell me."

"Grace said that if anyone tells the press, she'll have them locked up in the palace dungeon and tortured."

Liz took his hand, clasped it between both of hers, and looked into his eyes beseechingly.

"Okay, I will tell you what happened, and I don't expect anything in return—you don't even have to thank me. But if you do get a big story out of it, and you feel maybe that you've proved everything you have to prove, just remember, I'm waiting."

"Noted. Now, what's the story?"

"Matt McCloskey's wife's jewels have been stolen. It apparently happened a couple of days ago, probably while they were out to dinner, though she didn't notice they were missing until this morning, so it's possible the thief crept in, in the middle of the night."

"The necklace, the earrings?"

"Everything."

"Wow. A real-life cat burglar at Grace Kelly's wedding."

"I thought you'd like that. And there's more. This afternoon, apparently during the rehearsal for the wedding, the cat struck again and stole all of Marcee Pamp's jewelry."

"Incredible! Do you think it could be one of the guests?"

"Could be anybody who wasn't at the rehearsal."

The police were upstairs My father told my mother to wait downstairs, and he'd go and see what was going on and report back to her. He returned fifteen minutes later.

"Rainier doesn't trust the Monaco police to handle this, so he's brought in the New York City detective who guarded him when he was in New York."

"I don't suppose you got his name."

"Wrote it down right here." Jack showed her the writing on his cuff—Frank Cressi. "Cressi's going to interview all the guests and get them all to account for their whereabouts during the rehearsal."

"Do you think Matt will talk to me?"

"No, and I'm not going to tell Matt I told you, because I don't want him to get in trouble. And you have to promise not to breathe a word of this to other reporters."

"Oh, I think I can manage that."

*   *   *

134

Back at the croupier's apartment, Liz wrote the story and then called the palace for confirmation. She got some press attaché who denied the whole thing. But a little while later, there was a knock on the door, and my father came in.

"You're in big trouble."

"How do you mean?"

"Grace just called. She heard you'd called the palace, asking about the theft. Naturally she suspects me of being the security leak."

"Don't worry, a journalist never reveals her sources."

"It's put me in a slightly awkward situation now. The freedom of the press is a fine thing, but you don't necessarily want it in your own house."

The next day, newspapers all over the country splashed Elizabeth Toomey's exclusive across their front pages. Under headlines like ROBBERS SNATCH JEWELS OF GRACE'S BRIDESMAID and RIVIERA GANG STRIKES AGAIN AT REHEARSAL, readers learned "the victim of the latest robbery was Mrs. Marcee Pamp, Philadelphia, who reported all her jewels taken this afternoon from her room in the expensive Hôtel de Paris . . . the same hotel from which thieves stole $45,000 worth of jewels from wedding guest Matthew McCloskey . . . Prince Rainier called in New York City Detective Frank Cressi to help Monaco police halt the crooks who threaten to take away the guests' wealth from them even faster than the Monte Carlo gaming tables."

Grace and Rainier were furious. The word went out that there would be no more contact with the press until the wedding. But Elizabeth Toomey had her scoop—and it was her last one.

In September, the UP sent out an item that said, "Elizabeth Toomey, who writes the daily column 'Woman's View' for the United Press, will be married in New York City next month . . . Her recent assignments included covering the wedding of Grace Kelly and

Prince Rainier III, where she met the prospective bridegroom." In October she left the newspaper and gave up her career for family—in addition to me, there was my younger brother, Bruce. In later years, her talent found expression in writing captions for scrapbooks, a lot of wonderful letters, and more recently, e-mails, and a children's book with Jamie Wyeth called *Cabbages and Kings*. But she never wrote journalism again.

I met Princess Grace once, twenty-six years after the wedding of the century, in Hong Kong. I was there with my parents for the rechristening of the SS *Constitution*. The ship, which had stopped making transatlantic crossings in the 1960s, had been bought by a Chinese shipping magnate, C. Y. Tung, who planned to use it as a cruise ship in the Hawaiian Islands. In April 1982, he invited people from around the world to the ceremony, including my father, who by then was no longer in frozen food and knew C. Y. Tung through his current business, which also involved shipping. Princess Grace had agreed to attend the rechristening with Rainier, and to break the bottle of champagne over the *Constitution*'s bow.

The morning of the ceremony, just as we were about to leave our hotel, a sealed letter was delivered to the room. My father opened it, read it silently, and then said, "Good God."

"What is it?" said my mother, who had been fixing her hair in the mirror.

"It's from one of C.Y.'s sons," my father said, and then read the letter out loud. " 'Dear Jack and Liz, we regret to inform you that our beloved father passed away during the night. In view of this tragic event, the rechristening has been canceled and will be rescheduled at a later date.' "

As we were sitting there, shocked—for we had all seen C. Y. Tung the evening before, and he had seemed in excellent health—the telephone rang. It was Princess Grace calling, for my father. After talking about the news for a while, Grace said that under the circumstances, she ought not to be seen dining out in Hong Kong, but would the Seabrooks like to come to the Mandarin Hotel, to dine with Rainier and her in their suite?

"Do you think she's still mad about that story about the stolen jewels?" my mother asked as we were going up in the elevator to the Presidential Suite.

"She invited us," my father said. "She can't be that angry."

Grace greeted us, and if she was a little cool to my mother, she was very friendly toward and solicitous of me and wanted to hear all about Oxford University, where I was a student, and what I planned to do when I graduated. When I said I was interested in writing, perhaps journalism, Grace looked at my mother and smiled. "Well, if you inherited half your mother's talent," she said, "you should do very well."

Virtually every one of the young women attending Grace as bridesmaids had divorced by then. Both of her sisters were also divorced. Grace, of course, stayed married, but the Rainier I saw that night seemed distant. She regretted her decision to forgo her acting career and tried several times to find a way back to her old life, but could not overcome the objections of the palace and people of Monaco.

Then Grace said to my mother, "I remember you saying you would never give up your career for your family. But, unless I'm wrong, that's just what you did."

"Yes, I did," my mother said.

"And did you regret it?"

"Never for a moment," said my mother with a smile at me.

"Of course you didn't. How could you? How could any of us, really?"

When we parted that evening, it was with a promise to Grace that I would come to the palace that autumn, to meet her son Albert, who was about my age. But that never happened, because six months later, on September 14, 1982, Princess Grace was dead.

The *Constitution* cruised the Hawaiian Islands until the mid-1990s, when it was finally taken out of service and sold for scrap. On the way to the scrap yard, in the Far East, she began taking on water and sank about seven hundred miles north of Hawaii. She now rests on the bottom of the ocean, gone from sight, but still there. And that's how I feel about my parents' story now—it lies many years under the surface of the present, lost in the murky depths of family folklore, but I know from the peculiar currents it sometimes creates in my own marriage that it's still there, looming somewhere in the darkness.

Noises On

JAMES WOLCOTT

Movies from the fifties and early sixties made marriage troubles look like slow-drip dramas enacted behind drawn curtains, shadowed in secrecy and shame. A healthy front was preserved until the seams no longer held, and something snapped. Neighbors had no inkling anything was brewing with that nice couple down the lane until the patio party when the wife told him to go easy on the bourbon (the *look* he gave her!). Or maybe it was the young exec with money problems, joking about having macaroni and cheese for dinner two nights running, which got a snort from his poker buddies but provoked a row later, once he and his wife were alone. Pride carried a premium then. Even marital discord that climaxed with flying plates and kids cowering on the stairs would be graced with a gallant, forgiving fade-out, reflecting the protagonists' desire to keep up appearances for the sake of society, to carry one's head high out the door like Deborah Kerr into an uncertain, leaf-flickering tomorrow. Then community ranks would close, and the curtains would again draw shut.

It wasn't quite that way during my deformative years in the fifties and sixties. Marriage battles were waged in open daylight in living color. At full volume too, so that everybody could enjoy the latest installment. Few hothead couples bothered sweeping their problems under the linoleum in The Heights, as we called our little enclave in Maryland, northeast of Baltimore. Why it was called The

Heights remains a head-scratcher, because this low-rent housing project was strictly horizontal. These weren't the urban projects of high-rises, concrete courtyards, and corner liquor stores as fortified as Checkpoint Charlie; these were suburban tracts—strip apartments converted from WWII military housing, with all of the architectural charm and attention to detail that that conjures. Some residents made their hutches homey with floral trimmings and dabs of color (we weren't living on Tobacco Road), but for most it was a functional transient stop. Young couples and families on the way up, or singles and busted families on the way down. Losing face among the neighbors was a low-priority concern, since the gaggle next door might be gone next week, or your own family might up and move in the middle of the night one step ahead of the bill collectors or a sheriff's warrant, no time for tender adieux. I can vividly recall the summers there, Oriole afternoon games on the radio, BB-gun battles in the nearby woods, men and boys dragging cots out of their unair-conditioned apartments on the hottest evenings to sleep under the stars. Funny thing is, I can't remember the winters at all. Only the summers, when neighbors aired out their aggravations.

Sporadic infighting kept things hopping under our own roof, before and after we moved out of The Heights into an actual house with porch, haunted garage, the whole bit. The dialogue sometimes varied, but the sound effects were consistent: my parents' raised voices, punctuated by the rattle of car keys palmed off the kitchen table—slam of the screen door, slam of the car door—squeal of tires as the angrier of the two tore off to the American Legion or another of the fine drinking establishments along Route 40 (with free fistfights in the parking lots on weekends). One night, between jingle of keys and slammeth of door, my father ventured upstairs to make a dramatic announcement. This was unlike him, to take time out from a busy battle royal to address the junior partners. His voice was low and grave. "I'm leaving your mother, moving out of the house," he said. "Look after your brothers." I was the oldest of three brothers (another brother and sister would join the family album later). My father's tone carried such a toll of finality that one of the younger ones began crying as soon as the car left the driveway. And I remember assuring him in classic gruff-sergeant older-brother manner, *Ohhhh, he's not going anywhere, he'll be back, go to sleep.* My father wasn't given to bluffing; in his own mind he may have reached a grim decision, yet the precocious critic in me (I must have been eleven or twelve then) didn't buy his exit speech for a sec—he was hanging his words a little too heavy, overweighting them for scare effect. He had committed the crime of hokeyness. My parents murdering each other, sure, that I could believe back then. But divorce? Nah, never happen. And it never did. Forty-some years later, these two former combatants are still together, sober for more than two decades, and getting along better than they ever did, fond of each other in ways they never were before, back when the furniture seemed to levitate. Family get-togethers today are as calm as Quaker services. My parents didn't confront their demons, they outlasted them, tuckered them out. That wouldn't work for everybody, but it worked for them.

The same pattern holds for the rest of the clan, some of whose marriages once resembled mutual-destruction pacts—Apache dances without the dancing—while others seemed to grow moss up the sides through sheer mutual tedium. But then what bystander, even a close relative, knows what truly goes on inside anyone's marriage? Each marriage is a country unto itself, with its own lingo, customs, unwritten regulations, secret passwords, telepathic powers, and historical landmarks (the picnic table under the one shade tree at Denny's where they first held hands). All I know is that nearly all of the marriages in my family have so far gone the marathon distance. I have one uncle, he and his wife are in their eighties now. Last time my mother mentioned him I was amazed this uncle was still above earth. I figured this crusty character had long since been discontinued due to heavy taxation of the liver. Back in the day, this uncle's favorite form of greeting—which he extended to everyone, friends, strangers, and kids alike—was to flip his blunt middle finger. That was how he said hello. He could be driving by—you'd wave at him—he'd flip the bird. Little memories like that stay with you through the years. Today he's lame and near blind, as is his wife, both of them falling apart and yet *still together,* looking after each other as best they can. Hit after hit to their health, an accumulation of wreckage, and the two of them are still hanging tough. My brothers' and sister's marriages—they've all endured, a not unimpressive streak in our parcel of Maryland. At my ten-year high school reunion, I met former classmates who were already on their second merry-go-round ride, more than one of them informing me that the first marriage "didn't really count" because they had married young or impulsively (i.e., while drunk). They considered the second marriage a do-over.

My high school classmates married early. My parents married early. Their parents married early. My siblings and cousins married early. Their children married early. I married late. I played out the clock. I guarded my bachelorhood like the last Japanese sniper left on the island, putting up flurries of intense resistance between long spells of dolor, apathy, and hanging out at CBGB's. I had plenty of phony-baloney reasons for staying single, rationalizations galore. I fancied myself one of life's permanent bachelors, like the poet and librarian Philip Larkin, puttering in bookish privacy and grumbling at intruders. This wasn't a pose on my part (or his). I *liked* being alone. I prized solitude and the freedom to be a night owl, not having to keep anyone's hours but my own. Only later did I learn that England's poet of renunciation had juggled a pair of girlfriends like a going-to-pot roué in an Alan Ayckbourn farce, sacrificing himself to their interests only under duress. ("Monica has now moved in with Larkin, something never allowed before," recorded Anthony Powell in his journals. "Larkin, one of the most selfish men on earth, now spends all his time running up and down stairs with 'plates of warmed up spaghetti.'") Unlike my literary hero, I was a serial monogamist during my dating life, one woman being more than plenty for me to handle. But when it came to the big M-word, I acted equally unbudgeable. No wonder my girlfriends, one by one in a head-shaking succession, abandoned me to my lonely lounge sofa once they saw there was no future in the relationship. Or I would end the involvement, not wanting it to go any further, telling myself I was doing them a favor by not wasting any more of their time. After each breakup, I brooded (I'm dandy at that), beat up on myself (ditto), and submerged myself in work. I had a life, but it was limited, walled-in.

What was I holding on to, my coltish youth? What coltish youth? Since my teen years, I had been a walking advertisement for the adult-child syndrome, taking consolation in Benjamin Franklin's dictum that an old young man will become a young old man. Was I resistant to change? Was I ever. To friends who would tell me I was in a rut, I would quote in rebuttal Spencer Tracy's comment "I may be in a rut, but at least it's my rut," as if that were some gem of wisdom. But face it, there's no way to make a rut sound attractive. Did the holler fests I grew up hearing in Maryland make me marriage-shy? They sure didn't help, but I learned at any early age to tune out most of the noise. It was, of course, fear holding me back from the diving board—not the fear of commitment so much as the fear of failure. Somehow I had gotten into my head that I would flop as a husband, be a huge disappointment. I could accept failing myself. I'd failed myself in the past and knew that it wasn't a mortal weakness, much less a mortal sin. It was recoverable-from. But marriage meant failing someone else, failing in their eyes as well as my own, doubly condemned. Whoever I married was doomed to disappointment, I somehow convinced myself. You can convince yourself of anything if you put your morbid mind to it.

Fortunately, I found someone who extricated me from myself. If not, I dread to think what I might be now; a trifle moldy, that's for certain. My wife and I met at the sort of party Woody Allen staged in his midcareer movies before acute misanthropy leeched the social animal out of him. The setting: an Upper West Side apartment seasoned with *New Yorker* contributors and literary novelists who hung their commas with care. Two, three weeks earlier, while vacationing alone in Miami Beach, where I intended to complete the handwritten first draft of my first novel with a flourish (I tanned in the morning, scribbled in the afternoon), I suffered a dizzy spell. After sacking out for the evening, I lifted my head from the pillow— and everything spun sideways as if a film were running sideways through a projector. It was like having a whirlybird land inside my head. I thought maybe I had overdone the sun and figured the whirlies would pass. They didn't. Each new attack was announced by a pounding in my right temple that sounded like a fuzzy hammer activated by a trip wire. Unable to stand, I slid from the bed and crawled to the bathroom to throw up, the toilet bowl itself seeming to spin like an out-of-control satellite in space. It wasn't a dizzy spell, it was vertigo, dizziness to the nth degree. Ambulance— emergency room—tests. The initial diagnosis was Ménière's, more commonly known as swimmer's ear, but the tests were inconclusive. Extending my visit, I spent another ten days or so in Miami, released from the hospital once I was able to take two steps without falling and depositing myself back in the hotel, where I lay in bed and watched TV as if it were a portal into another dimension where nothing registered. Antivertigo medicine made the spinning stop, but I was unable to write a sentence or two without feeling queasy and having to lie down. After I was able to I return to New York (if I could have, I would have kissed the skyline), a second CAT scan in New York uncovered the real culprit, an inner-ear skin growth known as colesteatoma, which required surgery. When I asked what would happen if I opted not to have the operation, the specialist said, "Well, the growth could eventually migrate to the brain, at which point you'd have neurological problems, and you don't want those." No, sirree. I scheduled the operation, whose cost, along with my hotel and hospital expenses, would pillage my savings and max out my credit cards for years. A single man under forty, I had never gotten around to obtaining health insurance. In my professional as well as my personal life, I was freelancing.

The book party was my first outing since the whirlybird had landed, my first opportunity to get out of the apartment for weeks and remind myself what other people were like. I was woozy, depleted, deaf in one ear, tottering on a cane, feeling as fragile as a paper sack full of lightbulbs. I had to swivel my head sideways to hear anyone who was on my right side, and if I swiveled too abruptly, I became disoriented and had to brace against the nearest wall, if one was handy. I had to turn my head slowly and evenly, as if it were a tank turret. But I was still golden from the Florida sun, however, so I had that going for me. Taking it literally and gingerly one step at a time, I wasn't looking or hoping to meet anyone and start anything new, however. With the inner-ear surgery still some weeks away, my life was on hold. I was just trying to make it through the party without some slapstick mishap.

As I entered the apartment and began to negotiate a path toward some friendly, recognizable presence, I heard a male voice behind me inquire of his conversation partner, "Think it's AIDS?" My sudden weight loss and wooden cane lent itself to such speculation, particularly since AIDS anxiety was so pregnant in the air then, but the least he could have done is whisper; that's what whispering is for. I said howdy to a *Vanity Fair* colleague, who offered to introduce me to a film critic whose work I enjoyed. I tottered over, and with this critic was a gleamy-eyed, leggy woman with brunette bangs and a posture that made it seem as if she were poised on tiptoe even though she wasn't. She was an editor and dance critic. Laura and I made eye contact—her eyes seemed locked on me whenever we chatted—but I didn't let my imagination take any

145

bunny hops forward, calculating that she and the reviewer were probably dating, perhaps were even a steady duo. Besides, nice chats at parties are a dime a dozen. The party proceeded, mingle, mingle, and my legs began to feel leaden from standing for so long. I shared an elevator down with the reviewer and his date, and the three of us said our good-byes on the sidewalk on West End Avenue. As I pivoted with savoir faire to hail a taxi, my foot skidded and I stumbled, nearly crashing sideways into the trash receptacle on the corner. I assumed they witnessed this essay in elegance. Only later did I learn they had already turned away and were walking downtown, my pratfall unseen.

In my mind it was a pleasant encounter at a pleasant party, one of those one-off episodes in the city. But then we intersected at City Center for a Paul Taylor performance. Laura was there with a different escort (a fellow editor). I was on a blind date with an Australian blonde who later wrote a saucy book on the travails of dating and was probably making mental notes over dessert. I recognized Laura in the audience—we smiled hello—and at inter-mission, after Aussie blondie excused herself to stand in the inter-minable line for the ladies' room, Laura clicked-clicked up to me in the lobby as if she had a windup key in her back. We had another chat. Since I had been a ballet-goer since the seventies, I prided myself on being able to discuss dance without being a complete doofus, and it was clear to anyone within radius we were hitting it off. Not being bold enough to ask Laura for her number during intermission (taking another woman's phone number while your date is in the bathroom being a bit gauche), I had no way of taking advantage and following up on this small coincidence. Besides, the sexy Australian and I were really clicking. (Our first date turned out to be our last.) So I didn't bust a move.

Then came the third encounter. I was moseying along Central Park South, heading to the nearby Y to speak to a writers' class taught by a former girlfriend of mine, and at the corner was Laura in sweats, jogging in place while waiting for the traffic light to change, warming up for a run in the park. Now it was getting spooky. Three meetings in such a brief interval—fate seemed to be playing matchmaker, nudging us together like a yenta. I asked where I might reach her later, you know, maybe go out for dinner or something. My plan was to call her after the operation, assuming everything went okay. One possible side effect in removing the inner-ear growth, the surgeon had said, was the scalpel might ping the facial nerve, which could leave one side of my face permanently paralyzed. I wasn't sure how I'd feel if my face were half-stricken like a Batman villain, or how other people might feel about looking at it. But for once I didn't wait for events, something in me urged me to seize initiative, and I called Laura at her office and made a brunch date. Afterward, we went to a bad movie (*Cadillac Man,* for you cinema historians), which is always good conversation fodder, and kissed in the rain good-bye. Weeks later I underwent the operation and emerged with the facial nerve untouched but permanently deaf in one ear. When I was wheeled back to my hospital room, a bouquet was waiting for me. From Laura. And not just corner-bought flowers, but an elegant arrangement that showed taste, discernment. It was such a kind, generous, thoughtful gesture. I think I knew then I was a goner.

Oh, I put up a noble chicken fight. As we dated and discovered our symmetries (she was the oldest of five children, I was the oldest of five children, etc.), it became clear that we were meant to be together. Which didn't prevent me from trotting out all of my hobbled excuses against marriage, against even moving in together. Fear remained my ventriloquist, me its dummy. I wanted to get married, but I didn't want to *let* myself want it, to take the chance of, God forbid, being happy. Laura was unfazed. Cool, patient, steady. Playing her hand as brilliantly as Amarillo Slim. A chapter in her dusk-tinted novel *Women About Town* recounts the ultimatum she gave me that forced me to stop wobbling and make a

147

decision. I made the right one, one I've never regretted, aside from those stray, wincing moments when I rue what a sly, armor-piercing comedienne I married. Laura seemed so demure when we courted, so Mary Tyler Moore–ish with her bangs, black leggings, and wholesome bounce; little did I anticipate the raptures of humor she would have at my expense. The other great surprise was that after all those years of self-administered failure indoctrination, it turns out that I'm a *great* husband—affable, generous, gracious, easygoing, a good father to our three cats, handy around the apartment as long as you don't ask me to fix anything, and charming on social occasions that would break the morale of lesser men. The cliché is that a good marriage takes work, but the truth is that in most cases it takes work to make a good marriage go *bad*— real conscientious effort to foul it up. And, however I pretend to portray myself, I'm not that big a fool.

Man Finds His Voice

JOHN BURNHAM SCHWARTZ

A picture that comes to mind when I think of meeting my wife is this: a tall, lighted window on the fifth floor of an apartment building on the rue Monge in Paris. It is the middle of the night. And by the middle of the night I mean, specifically, that Pacific island of an hour when on either side of you the day feels, indeed is, too far removed to touch; too far even to remember.

Look in that window, now. As if, say, you are observing this strange, floating scene from the fifth floor of the identical building across the street—a dentist's office, as it happens, closed for business. Sit in the empty, vinyl-clad hydraulic chair, in the darkness faintly illumined by stainless steel implements, and take an interest in what you're seeing twenty-five yards away: the double windows opening onto a terrace deep enough only for a single chair (though no chair is visible); the odd lack of curtains or shades; the sparsely furnished white room with walls glowing from a single, tiny halogen bulb. A chest of drawers in one corner; on the floor, a contemporary patterned rug; at the back of the room, a simple wooden bed. An IKEA of the spirit. The lamp a slender black flamingo dipping its neck over the bed, on which a young man wearing nothing but boxer shorts, with a borrowed paperback of John Fowles's *The Magus* cracked open on his chest, lies in a fitful, not quite unconscious state somewhere between sleep and psychosis.

149

This is me on the night before I met my wife. It is June 1991 and I am twenty-six years old.

I say met my wife, but in fact I'd met my wife a few months earlier, at a party in Cambridge, Massachusetts, on my last night of a semester spent teaching Harvard undergraduates. The Gulf War was on. Aleksandra was still a college junior, all of twenty (and, for the record, not my student): I thought her the loveliest and smartest of a roomful of lovely, smart young women. She seemed to have traveled everywhere at a ridiculously young age. She spoke French and was preternaturally well read—by which, given my concerns of the moment, I suppose I meant not that she had read Austen and Balzac and Woolf (she had), but that she had also happened to have read my own first novel, published two years earlier. I learned that she had spent part of her childhood in Paris, where her parents still lived and where I'd been living for more than a year. The conversation ended with her giving me their phone number and suggesting we might see each other over there sometime. Then I returned to my temporary rooms, packed my bags, and by next evening—Valentine's Day, with bombs falling over Iraq—was on a plane back to Europe.

Now it seems reasonable to wonder, as I didn't feel comfortable wondering then, what sort of person my future wife had encountered that evening at a party in Cambridge. Or, more accurately, how did that person *appear* to her on first acquaintance? Because the person she would meet again in Paris just a few months later, and, whether on that very day or on the days to come, to whom she would generously commit her most private heart, was in many ways a fundamentally changed person; the same, maybe, yet so frayed at the edges as to be more or less unrecognizable to himself.

It was snowing the morning I reached Paris. Out the taxi window, the city appeared gray, foreign, inanimate. I lugged my bags up the five flights of stairs, my footsteps echoing through the old stone building: there was no one here I knew. My apartment

150

was freezing. The refrigerator was empty. I went to bed with my socks on and slept all day. I remember that sleep because it was one of the last periods of rest, save for more than a few alcohol-induced stupors, that I would experience for quite a while.

The panic attacks I began to suffer on my return to Paris were not the first I had experienced, but they arrived with far greater frequency than in the past. At first they were tightly focused on the question of my writing—whether the second novel I'd been diligently working on for the past year was good enough, or any good at all. I suspected a negative answer—how strangely satisfying now to have been so prescient—and the unarticulated fear of it began to haunt me like a dead man walking. Wherever I went, I heard lifeless footsteps behind me, and they were my own. This was unpleasant, to be sure, though not completely unprecedented, and so at some level still manageable. What writer doesn't have doubts about his talent, especially after a surprising early success? (The reception of my first book, *Bicycle Days,* had far outstripped my hopes for it, not to mention my shallow reserves of self-belief.)

It didn't help that I felt I had few people to talk to at the time. I had enjoyed a small group of close friends in Paris, Americans mostly, but in the last few months they had all decamped for other countries. In their absence, like any desperate animal, I availed myself of what consolation was on hand.

At two o'clock one morning, panicked to the tips of my fingers by the certainty that I was and would always be a failure, I phoned a woman I had slept with a couple of times but otherwise hardly knew. Groggily perplexed, if not alarmed, by my impromptu call— to say nothing of the maniacal warp to my voice—she bravely offered to let me spend the rest of the night at her place. I was at her building practically before she could hang up, taking the stairs to her apartment two at a time. Soon I'd slipped into bed beside her.

151

She was already fading back to sleep—no doubt in the hope that I was just a bad dream and would be gone with the daylight—while, awake in the darkness, I shut my eyes and tried to convince myself that the real reason I had come was for this shared bodily proximity, and not my unappeasable terror.

Later in the night, finding me sitting at the foot of the bed with my head in my hands, she drowsily inquired if anything was wrong. I told her I was anxious about the novel I was writing, about whether it was really any good at all. For a few long moments she said nothing. Then she sighed, rolled over, and reluctantly asked me what my book was about.

As I told her the plot, I kept my back to her and my head in my hands. Because she knew hardly anything of the work I'd been doing, I had to start my narrative from the beginning, which made it long and tedious and finally confusing, even to me; especially to me. My voice was a painful droning until it stopped, somewhere in the middle of fictitious events, after not much had happened and even less had been revealed. We sat in unvarnished silence as the night lengthened like a mirror tilted to reveal a barren, moonless sky. Ahead of schedule, it seemed, I had reached a dead end in my own story, had glimpsed the truth that this woman was a stranger to me and that I myself was less than nothing, a figment of my own wasted imagination.

My condition worsened over the next couple of months. My anxiety lost its pinpoint focus on my writing, grew formlessly expansive, voracious, until finally it began to break down the soft, naked core of my self. Internal walls crumpled like paper, leaving every idea I'd ever had vulnerable to annihilating negation. A sense of absolute aloneness in a vast universe took hold, and with it an unbearable terror of death, which in turn drove my exhausted mind into a dank cave of dangerous morbidity. That these and similar feelings were obvious clichés of a kind, familiar to millions, only increased my despair: I could not seem to be original even in collapse.

Bit by bit I became afraid of the dark. Lights would be extinguished, and wherever I happened to be—at home, in a theater, riding the Métro—within seconds an awareness of my debilitated psychological state would rise up and encircle me like a noose, and the room would start to whirl, suggesting oblivion. After an afternoon showing of (what else?) Woody Allen's *Bananas,* during which the projector temporarily broke down and the small Left Bank cinema in which I sat was thrown into blackness for perhaps two minutes, I was so unnerved that I stopped going to the movies altogether.

I began to drink wine from dusk until early morning, when, the halogen light in my bedroom forever shining, I would pass out for an hour or two, before the sun and the sounds of traffic would enter my thin, unshrouded windows and rouse me back to consciousness. It was not thoughts of suicide that frightened me then, but a recognition of something weaker and more shameful: a draining away while still alive.

That spring I made friends with an older American novelist and his wife. They would invite me to their apartment on the rue des Saints Pères for long drunken lunches with a varied group of wildly gregarious journalists. Their invitations afforded me one of my few effective means of temporarily keeping my panic at bay, and I always accepted. Once established in their spacious, smoke-filled rooms, I always drank a great deal and sometimes stayed on through dinner (I even did the dishes once, after my hosts had gone to bed). On one of those blurry occasions, early in June, I saw Aleksandra for the second time.

The living room was crowded with people and ringing with laughter. She entered alongside her parents—the same good people whose phone number, in a fit of doubt, I had thrown away months

153

before without ever dialing. I watched her scan the room, recognize me in surprise, and stop. I have little recollection of what was said from that point on; only of her pale, smiling face framed by dark brown hair looking up at me. I see her father's face too, pale as a moonbeam, and her mother's. That is all. The sound of her voice, but not the words. A sense, somehow, of a door being knocked on, and of a light appearing like a sudden flame on the other side.

A few evenings later, I went to dinner for the first time at her parents' apartment. A dusky, incipient moon hung over the Place Saint-Sulpice as I walked into the sixth arrondissement and turned up the rue du Cherche-Midi. It was the hour when normally I might have begun to feel the stirrings of panic, but tonight I found myself thinking about Aleksandra instead.

She opened the door wearing red jeans and black boots and a black, short-sleeve sweater. Behind her stood an enormous dog, a Bouvier des Flandres. Fortunately, he stopped barking (at crotch level) when he saw that she was pleased to see me.

From that evening I carry two memories in particular. The first is nothing more than standing alone with her in the kitchen and testing strands of cooked spaghetti from the pot to see if they are done. The second is sitting beside her on the sofa, a book of photographs of Normandy open on our laps; and the pulsing sensation of my hand, pressed down by the weight of the book, resting hidden against her outer thigh.

There is also the overall impression her parents made on me that evening—which, I suppose, gives some indication of the impression that I must have made on them. They could not have been more gracious to me or stood less on ceremony. They struck me as witty, smart, engagingly eccentric, and thoroughly trusting of their daughter's ability to handle herself in the company of would-be suitors—of which, clearly, I was not the first. They seemed unconcerned by, or perhaps just unaware of, the recent instability of my mind. But then they were both writers themselves—one the European correspondent for *The New Yorker,* the other an anthropologist—and so, I reasoned, could be counted on for a certain degree of insanity themselves. From that first evening on, their apartment came to feel like a haven to me, where I might let down my emotional guard without fear of being judged. The following month, in fact, after Aleksandra had left France and I had risen a few notches further on the nut meter, I would pass quite a few lifesaving afternoons reading in their garden, sometimes talking to them and sometimes not, while they went about their business, as if I were already a member of the family.

I had dinner there happily once more in the next few days. This time I brought my stepfather, a poet, who had just flown all the way from his home in Hawaii to check on me, and to make sure that I wasn't going to do something stupid to myself. Dozens of late-night phone calls and rambling letters had no doubt given him and my mother a more informed picture of my current psychiatric condition than I'd intended. As it happened, he and Aleksandra's mother were longtime admirers of each other's work; everyone quickly became friends, and the evening, even to my somewhat erratic perceptions, glowed with a sense of intimate promise.

Then life resumed. The next day, as planned, my stepfather and I took the train south to the Lot, where for many years he'd owned an old stone farmhouse. We stayed there ten days, gardening and reading and talking, while I struggled to keep afloat on a briefly becalmed tide of panic. I could see that he was trying hard to shore me up, and when I could feel anything at all, I was deeply moved by his efforts. He had brought with him—as I imagined a Sant Bernard might carry a flask of brandy to a skier buried in an avalanche—a bottle of Xanax prescribed by a friend. But in those days neither of us knew the first thing about antianxiety medication—this was still, relatively speaking, the dinosaur age of psychopharmacology for the general consumer—and despite my continued, nerve-racked insomnia, I declined to take any of the pills. Of course, I had no such

155

reservations about continuing my nightly downing of a bottle of Cahors, followed by a glass or two of plum eau-de-vie.

The narrow, claustrophobia-inducing second bedroom, with its sharply sloping roof and two single beds placed head-to-head, had several times, in the fifties, been slept in by my stepfather's friends and fellow poets Sylvia Plath and Ted Hughes. Maybe it was their raving, haunted spirits that kept me awake despite my faithful boozing. In any event, in the country as in the city, my nights were long and weird.

Probably the most curative thing my stepfather did for me during our time together down south, aside from simply keeping me company, was to repeatedly bring up the subject of Aleksandra. He has always adored her. Out of the blue he kept announcing what a lovely young woman she was, while shooting me a look that declared I'd be worse than a fool if I let her slip away. It was enough, coming from him, a man I loved and admired—to say nothing of how well I knew he'd always done with the ladies—to intermittently rouse me out of anxious navel-gazing and into serious thoughts of a possible relationship.

She was gone by the time I got back to Paris—to a summer film course in New York, and then to Harvard for her final year. All was not lost, however: during the spring I had made plans to leave Paris and settle permanently in Cambridge, where I would teach again. So the stars were seemingly aligned for us, after all—yet, somehow, not: back once more in my curtainless apartment on the rue Monge, without either my stepfather or Aleksandra to talk to, I quickly descended to a new level of mental instability. The days were an obstacle course of quicksand swamps and hidden trapdoors; the nights like one long, hellish summer in Finland. The internal weather, to paraphrase W. C. Fields, was fit for neither man nor beast.

When I wasn't writing pages of execrable fiction (I was nothing if not dogged in my literary efforts, I must say that much for my younger self), I was engaged in the metaphorically apt task of deconstructing my physical life in Paris: searching for someone to take over the lease on my apartment, and trying to sell or loan my sparse collection of IKEA furniture. It was a lonely, depressing job, this dismantling of an existence that two years earlier, flush from the success of my first novel, I had embarked on with such excitement. In the end, typically for me at that time, I panicked and wound up leaving everything in return for a hastily scrawled promissory note from an Irish couple I'd never met, who seemed unlikely to ever find the means to make good the debt; and, indeed, I have never seen a cent of that money.

During this strained, inglorious last month (A Moveable Feast it wasn't), Aleksandra's parents offered me my only real refuge. Several afternoons a week I would sit in their garden, like Hans Castorp after a binge, reading a long, depressing novel (I can't remember what novel it was, only that it was long and infinitely depressing) or, more likely, talking to Jane, between her bouts of writing, while Vincent, between *his* bouts of writing, watered the roses nearby. Every so often Jane would say something provocative about French politics or some book they'd both read—and Vincent would calmly interject, "No, Jane," and continue his watering. I found it all remarkably soothing. And so my final weeks in Paris passed.

It was a not entirely human being traveling under my passport who limped into JFK one steamy night in late July. I dropped my bags in my aunt's apartment downtown, downed a couple of drinks, and made an emergency appointment with a psychophar-macologist for the next day. Then I called Aleksandra and told her that her parents and I had become friends while she'd been away.

She replied that she already knew; they'd told her all about it.

Our first official date, two nights later, at a Japanese restaurant on Columbus Avenue, coincided with my second day of taking the

antidepressant imipramine. The pills could not have started working yet, but I didn't know that at the time. By then I was pretty
worked up about the whole idea that I was "sick" and needed
medicine—though clearly I *was* sick and needed medicine, as well as
a good kick in the head—and without much fight I gave in to the
questionable impulse to tell Aleksandra all about it over dinner.
Not exactly the sort of first-date banter from which hall of fame
lovers are made. But then Aleksandra, with her own eccentric
family, had already shown herself to be nearly immune to my
odd tics of behavior and my nerves as electrified as a barnyard
fence. She listened to my story of epic self-absorption with rapt
attention and perhaps even a dollop of implied sexual compassion;
and then we walked uptown to her apartment. We ended up lying
on her bed watching a tape of *It Happened One Night*. And it *did*
happen that night, I'm glad to report. Eventually, we fell asleep.

When I awoke, it was four in the morning, and I had two
epiphanies in succession. The first was that I was in bed with this
beautiful, sexy, remarkable woman. The second was that I had not
brought my medication with me. It is an indication of just how far I
had fallen from the modest plateau of sanity that the second
epiphany somehow managed to trump the first. My face grew
hot. I tried to go back to sleep but it was no use. Aleksandra opened
her eyes to find me already dressed and whispering about forgotten
pills and rogue panic attacks and what a good time I'd had but why,
so sorry, I had to leave.

She was away for August and I didn't see her, though we spoke on
the phone a couple of times. In early September, I drove her up to
Cambridge in a rented car loaded to the roof with our belongings.
We were both nervous and a little awkward with each other. We
knew a good deal more of each other's history and personality than
we had at the start of the summer. But where France had seemed a
separate place, a kind of visitation, the journey that day, in its

mundane purposefulness—I was driving her up so she could start school and I could start my job—felt weightier, and at the same time uncertainly settled.

Then, halfway there, something unexceptional occurred that made us both feel more comfortable. From the highway we saw a sign that said FOOD AND BOOKS and decided to stop there for lunch. True to advertising, as we paid the check, we were allowed to take a secondhand book from a shelf of titles patrons had left over the years. We jointly chose an old jacketless hardcover of Wallace Stegner's *Angle of Repose.* The book sits on a shelf in our house now—as does, in a different room, an empty bottle of champagne from the night of our engagement five years later.

In Cambridge, I moved into the second floor of a handsome nineteenth-century house on Brattle Street. My own little sanatorium. What Aleksandra found over at chez Schwartz that autumn was perhaps not what your average college senior—or nursing home resident, for that matter—would have bargained for.

There were some positive signs of activity on the homefront, it's true. My teaching was going well; and having wisely jettisoned the Parisian roman à clef, I was contemplating the start of another new novel. More significantly, I had begun seeing a pychoanalyst four times a week, at whose suggestion I'd added a small dose of Klonopin (an antianxiety medication) to my present intake of imipramine. The cumulative effect of these actions was to at least put a floor under my twitching feet; to stop the falling. And as the falling ceased, my vision grew less distorted and gradually I was able to gain a better view of Aleksandra, and she of me. For both of us during those first months in Cambridge a kind of watchful patience necessarily set in; a helpless, but by no means hopeless, waiting for the growth of intimacy.

Certainly, this was different from the evolution of so many romantic relationships I know of (including any number of my own failed attempts pre-Aleksandra), in which intimacy, or some simulacrum of it, is the easy part, the rabbit out of the gate, and patience with each other's nature is the virtue that must be learned, slowly and sometimes painfully, down the bumpy line of years. We are creatures, all of us, of more than mere habit; we are creatures of experience. But experience is not always, or even often, the stuff of bells and whistles, to say nothing of best-selling memoirs. So much of experience is quiet, nearly invisible. It might take the form of waiting, half-unaware, for the first sign of a change of season; of an exploratory, wordless leaning into mutual passion.

All the same, I wouldn't want to give the impression that Aleksandra and I enjoyed a smooth and neurosis-free autumn that year. How boring that would be. The truth was that Aleksandra was Job, only much better looking. My extreme reticence at home—between analysis, medication, teaching, writing, the whole nine yards, I was left drained and virtually speechless, a human husk, by dinnertime—would have been rough going even on a monk; and my girlfriend, I must add, was no monk. The situation would have affected even the strongest of egos. In Aleksandra's case, the stress understandably manifested itself in a growing obsession with my analyst: she began to imagine that she saw him everywhere, a Freudian Zelig, even though she didn't know what he looked like. We would go grocery shopping at Star Market and she would come rushing up, grab me by the arm, and declare, "I think I just saw Dr. Dugan by the broccoli!" And I would have to break it to her that it was not my analyst she had seen, but the stock boy.

And then, at Christmas, I left town for a month to visit my family in Hawaii. Outwardly it was a quiet trip, as quiet as the autumn had been. I spent most of it reading on the beach. Inwardly, however, I was beginning to hear voices. Not the panicked voices that still occasionally haunted me from my time in Paris, but voices at once new and resonantly familiar. It was Aleksandra I heard, and myself. We were talking to each other, holding intimate conversations that in reality had not yet taken place but which, inside me now, were already occurring with indelible meaning. And with the sound of her voice came countless tactile images of her, her curves and scent and skin, and a sudden, powerful awakening of my passion.

Many aspects of our relationship intensified dramatically upon my return to Cambridge. I won't describe them all here—suffice it to say that most involved the enthusiastic laying on of hands. More notable even than the physical, though, was that I finally began to speak openly of my feelings for her, and one of the first things I said was that I loved her. Not long afterward, I asked her to move in with me, and she agreed.

All of which indicated a change in our relationship profound enough that Aleksandra ended up giving it its own title. Man Finds His Voice was how she aptly described that period in our lives. Nearly thirteen years later, long free of psychopharmaceuticals and daily aware of my good fortune, I think the title is still a good one. Man—or this man, anyway—is still happily finding his voice. As he should be. For who can fathom the illogical reasons, the terrifying depths of commitment, the brazen farsightedness that might lead a whole person to passionately bind her soul to a broken one? I am here today to tell you that I was once the recipient of such a bestowal, which can only be called love.

Conversion

JONATHAN MAHLER

Who doesn't love a bris? Or so I was thinking a couple of years ago, when I brought along my non-Jewish girlfriend to the apartment of some friends to watch their newborn son go under the knife.

Jews have been circumcising their sons since biblical times. The ritual began with Abraham and Isaac and has spanned countless countries and generations. As such, a bris makes for a rare moment in life when you can't help but feel connected to something larger, more meaningful. What better way to introduce Danielle to the transcendent appeal of Judaism?

Imagine the scene. It's a sunny November morning and about forty people are gathered in the living room of a classic six in Park Slope, Brooklyn. On center stage we have our infant, lying unsuspectingly on a pillow in the lap of his maternal grandfather. The master of ceremonies, a bearded man in a black suit and skullcap known as a mohel, hovers above, preparing to fulfill God's will. The *mohel* leans down, Mogen clamp in hand, and the room falls silent. Another link in the long chain of the Jewish people is about to be forged. The excitement is building. We are not just witnesses but participants in this reaffirmation of our covenant with God. The father looks understandably tense. The mother is starting to weep.

Of course, I'd noticed the crying mother at previous *brit milot* (plural for *bris*), but to me that was always part of the pageantry. I look over at Danielle expecting to see her caught up in the drama, maybe even tearing up a bit herself. She isn't even watching! I tap her on the shoulder and she turns toward me. She is, quite obviously, horrified. "This is barbaric," she mutters.

The freshly cut baby begins wailing, the mohel makes kiddush, and the crowd starts singing "Siman Tov U'mazel Tov." Now it's time to eat. For the past eight days, I had been talking up the tribal feast that would follow the tribal rite—the bagels and lox, the whitefish salad, the pickled herring. In a cruel gesture that I can hardly fail to notice, Danielle passes over the array of smoked fish and settles on the coffee cake instead.

Another affronted Jew put it best: *Am I not human? Do I not bleed?*

My history with Danielle began long before we ever met.

During the mideighties I attended Deerfield Academy, a prep school in western Massachusetts where her father was a dean and her mother a teacher, my sophomore English teacher in fact. Deerfield has since gone coed, but back then it was all boys—550 of them, between the testosterone-soaked ages of fourteen and eighteen. Danielle and her sister rarely, if ever, showed their faces on campus, but it was known that the Mattoons had daughters. There had even been some sightings. They were rumored to be blond. And attractive.

Danielle resurfaced in my life in the late nineties, when we were both working at a magazine in New York (me as a writer, she as an editor). I saw something auspicious in the coincidence; she did not. Over the years, Danielle had received more than her share of advances from Deerfield boys, who she invariably suspected were acting out some latent crush on her mother. Not that such advances made much of an impression on her. Deerfield tends to breed a certain type: clean-cut, polite, athletic. Her tastes ran in a shaggier, more eccentric direction.

Fortunately, I was not your typical Deerfield boy. Among other things, I was Jewish. And in time, after a few late-night edits and countless reassurances about the nature of my intentions—*You don't even look like your mother*—I succeeded where many of my fellow alumni had failed.

Dating a non-Jew should not, at least in theory, have been an issue for me. My parents, while both Jewish, were fairly secular. When I was an infant, they left New York City for the distinctly un-Jewish town of Palm Springs, California, a land of rich retirees, meticulously manicured country clubs, and palm-lined streets named after aging celebrities—Bob Hope Drive, Frank Sinatra Way. The local Reform temple where I was bar mitzvahed—it was around the corner from Liberace's house—didn't provide much of a counterpoint to the materialism that bloomed all around us. (Put it this way: the rabbi collected antique cars.)

I don't want to give the wrong impression; my parents were proud of their religious heritage. They gave generously to Jewish charities and took the family to Israel, and the ashtray on my mother's night table sat on a stack of Holocaust histories, which she devoured like romance novels. But unlike my maternal grand-parents, who kept a strictly kosher home, my parents, like so many second- and third-generation Jewish immigrants, had drifted away from observant Judaism.

As an adult, I continued along the same path toward assimilation with one small detour: in my midtwenties I worked at a weekly Jewish newspaper called the *Forward*. This may sound like an attempt to get in touch with my Jewish identity. It wasn't. I took the job at the *Forward* because it was an exciting newspaper, and because I was desperate to stop covering business. If anything, I was wary about getting stuck in the Jewish-journalism ghetto. And as it turned out, working at the *Forward* made it easier for me to ignore my own religious identity. Any unexpressed desire to express my Jewishness was satisfied by going to work every day.

164

And anyway, by the time I started seeing Danielle, the *Forward* was in my past.

From the first time I brought Danielle home, my parents set about making her feel comfortable in our—relatively speaking, anyway—Jewish home. On Rosh Hashanah, one of the three days a year that my family spends in synagogue, my mom told Danielle that she looked tired, and that if she didn't feel up to it, she should stay home. At lunch that afternoon, my mom, always on the lookout for even the smallest disqualifier, barely seemed to notice when Danielle passed along the bowl of gefilte fish without spearing a piece. My Jewish mother seemed to like my shiksa girlfriend; I should have been thrilled. Somehow, I wasn't.

Danielle and I got more serious. As we did, something strange started happening, something that got me thinking again about my Jewish identity. I can trace the first sign of it back to a warm afternoon in Brooklyn. I had just done a lap around Prospect Park and was walking home when a couple of cheerful Hasidic teenagers in black suits and fedoras accosted me. "You Jewish?" they asked.

As odd as it may sound to non–New Yorkers, this is a relatively common occurrence in the city, particularly in Brooklyn. I had been approached by young Lubavitcher proselytizers at least a dozen times before and had never given them more thought than I would a Hare Krishna slapping a tambourine. This time, I stopped and answered yes. Before I knew it, I was wrapping my sweaty arm in tefillin—small holy boxes that are bound to the body with leather straps during prayer—for the first time since my bar mitzvah.

A few weeks later, I found myself driving around Brooklyn looking for challahs on a Friday afternoon. The next day, standing in line at the butcher shop, I spotted the thick-cut pork chops, my favorite quick and dirty weeknight dinner, and opted for lamb instead. Now in the scheme of things, these are, admittedly, modest life adjustments. But the funny thing was that while I was tentatively dipping my toes into deeper Jewish observance, when it came to Danielle, I professed to be diving in headlong. And so there I was, spending a Saturday in front of my computer, only to come home and extol the salutary effects of honoring God's command to preserve a day for rest.

A psychoanalyst would have told me that I was overcompensating for my feelings of guilt about dating a non-Jew. The yawning hole in this assessment is that my parents—the preeminent source of guilt in my life—approved of Danielle. In fact, they were hoping we'd get married.

Looking back now, it all seems so clear. Religious faith tends to ebb and flow like the tide. One generation advances toward it, the next retreats from it. I was beginning to creep closer to Judaism. The only problem was, I was also falling in love with a woman whose father was named Skip.

It's a simple paradox, even if I was unable to see it at the time. And so, after a lifetime of feeling perfectly comfortable surrounded by gentiles, I suddenly felt like an embattled minority. I fed my growing paranoia by surfing the Web sites of various Jewish organizations for the latest studies on the "continuity crisis"—their preferred term for the rising rates of intermarriage in America. There seemed to be no way around it: I was a traitor to my people, and nothing drove the point home quite so powerfully as Christmas at the Mattoons'.

Danielle's parents had always been warm toward me. My ethnic heritage and cultural orientation notwithstanding, I was in many ways a more familiar breed to them than the non-Jews whom Danielle had bought home before me, which is another way of saying that I drank beer and played team sports. Simply put, there were no signs that the Mattoons were at all uncomfortable with my being Jewish. There was even a familial precedent for Danielle's straying from the Episcopal Church. In the early seventies, when her parents were young professors at the University of Michigan,

Danielle's mother had taken up Zen Buddhism and has been practicing it ever since.

And yet, when we set out from Brooklyn for the Mattoons' home in rural Connecticut for my first Christmas, I felt as though I were heading toward enemy territory. Danielle and I were both silent as we drove over the Triborough Bridge and north through the Bronx listening to Coldplay. No doubt Danielle was thinking about her Christmases past. I was certainly thinking nostalgically about mine: those afternoons spent eating Chinese and going to the movies with my fellow Jews.

Two hours later we were in snow-encrusted New England pulling up the long driveway to their white-shingled house. It was a postcard picture of Christmas, complete with candles in the windows and a green wreath on the door. I did not feel well. Danielle's parents and sister came out to greet us. I smiled weakly.

We made our way inside and my eyes quickly found the tree. The Christmas tree. With presents for me no less. And as if my betrayal of the Jewish people weren't already manifestly clear, dangling from one of the branches was an ornament with my name on it.

A little later in the day—sometime after ham was consumed—I stopped Danielle in front of the tree to express my horror. I wasn't quite sure what to say, a fact that soon become evident.

"Don't they know I'm Jewish?" I sputtered, stabbing my finger at the offending object.

"Oh, relax," she told me. "It's a snowman, not a crucifix."

"But it's a *Christmas* ornament," I tried vainly to explain.

If I could have ended the relationship there, I would have. But it was too late. I was already in love. What's more, the truth was that Danielle was perfectly suited to me. I'm not talking about the blond hair and willowy figure. She was an expert at dealing with my neuroses and she seemed constitutionally incapable of nagging.

And so I launched my conversion campaign.

I would like to say now that I introduced the idea subtly,

imperceptibly, in the spirit of, say, Mr. Miyagi in *The Karate Kid*. In truth, my approach was more *Great Santini*. Knowing that Danielle had developed an interest in Jewish day schools—because, as she put it, they seemed "so anti-touchy-feely"—I informed her that they were off-limits to children born of non-Jewish mothers. Then, wrapping up a phone conversation one afternoon, I wondered aloud if she was aware that if we were married and she didn't convert, we couldn't be buried in the same cemetery.

Not surprisingly, Danielle wasn't ready to plunge into the mikvah bath, but she was willing to trek up to the 92nd Street Y to register for a six-month Introduction to Judaism class. It was a start.

Leading us into an office cluttered with miscellaneous Judaica, the rabbi sat us down for a casual pro forma interview. He and I knew some people in common from my days at the *Forward* and we chatted for a few minutes about them while Danielle listened in silence. Then, out of the blue, he turned toward her and propped his elbows on one of his crossed knees.

"So, Danielle," the rabbi asked, "how would you describe your Jewish identity?"

It would have been a tough question for most Jews to handle. Danielle looked at him blankly. "What do you mean?"

"Well," the rabbi said, presumably attempting to clarify, "how would you describe your relationship to Judaism?"

Danielle pointed at me. "Him. He's my relationship to Judaism."

A long pause followed. "Well," the rabbi finally said, straining to sound optimistic, "I guess that's something."

"Jew school," as Danielle had soon taken to calling it, consisted of mostly interfaith couples, engaged or soon-to-be engaged, navigating their paths to marriage. Each class was two hours long, with a break for a (kosher) snack in the middle. During the first hour, one of the students would present an analysis of a passage from the Torah. During the second half, the rabbi—happily not the one who had interviewed us—would discuss a Jewish ritual.

168

The first couple of months were rocky. The Torah was far more violent than I remembered, and I suspected that Danielle, who averts her eyes during action movies, was not having an easy time stomaching the wholesale destruction of entire biblical villages. I had also underestimated how much of the Torah is devoted to God ennobling the struggles of his chosen people, which also didn't exactly strike a chord with her.

Among our classmates was an elfin, muscular, Polish-born avid cyclist named Ira, whose mother was a Holocaust survivor. Ira's fiancée, Kathleen, was blond, freckled, and athletic and came from a big Irish Catholic family. She was in her late thirties or early forties. Having children was important to both of them, and they had ended and resumed their relationship several times over religious issues. Ira's mother refused to speak to Kathleen.

As the class progressed, Ira emerged as our most feverishly committed student, bringing in photocopied articles on the return of anti-Semitism in America and reporting weekly on the latest synagogue he and Kathleen had auditioned.

For a while, I cheered him on as he fought the good fight. Over time, though, as I watched Ira nudge his shy girlfriend to volunteer for the weekly Torah commentary, much as a father might prod his scared child to swim into the deep end of the pool, my allegiances began to shift.

Self-recrimination quickly followed. With my passive-aggressive references to cemeteries and Jewish day schools, was I any better? Among the things I admired most about Danielle was the graceful modesty with which she lived her life. Naturally it felt indecent to her to glom on to someone else's harrowing history.

Near the end of the course, I decided it was time to fashion a compromise. We would have a Jewish wedding and bring up our children Jewish, but the conversion question would remain open.

We raised our chuppah on a July evening on the greensward of the Hotchkiss School, the New England prep school where Danielle's parents now work. I studied the skies nervously all day, fearing we'd have to put the backup plan—the school's "nondenominational" chapel—into effect. But the rain held off, and during the reception, while watching Skip bounce gamely on a chair hoisted high above the dance floor, I made my peace with my future. Things had turned out pretty well.

A few weeks after we returned from our honeymoon, Danielle came home from work one Friday evening with candles and a couple of challahs. (Granted, it was after dark and she had already taken a bite or two out of one of them, but she did get the day right.) She announced that she wanted to try to make Shabbat dinners as often as possible.

Naturally I was stunned, but over the next couple of days it slowly came into focus for me. During those six months of Jew school, as I psychoanalyzed Ira and Kathleen and worried obsessively about how Danielle was taking to the Torah, she was starting to find her own route into Judaism via its religious rituals. So many Jewish prayers are about sanctifying the everyday—this was something she could relate to.

A little over a year later, Danielle was pregnant and Christmas was again upon us. Under the tree was a gift for her from her sister, a book about raising Jewish children called *The Blessings of a Skinned Knee*. The philosophy was in many ways the exact inverse of what you might expect. The stereotypical Jewish mother is overprotective, indulgent, prone to living vicariously through the achievements of her children. But this book argued that, at bottom, raising a Jewish child is in fact about ensuring that there will be someone around to honor God and try to make the world a better place after his or her parents are gone. Danielle was soon quoting from it.

Any fantasies I had about my wife suddenly deciding to zealously abide by the letter of Jewish law—and believe me, I had them—were soon banished when she announced that a friend was throw-

170

ing her a baby shower. (Jewish custom prohibits acknowledging the impending arrival of a child.) Once again, a compromise was reached. She would have the shower but gifts would be discouraged, and she certainly wouldn't open any until after the baby was born.

I picked Danielle up after the shower. Now eight months pregnant, she tottered toward the car carrying two heavy shopping bags. This was not a good sign. Driving home, I asked, warily, how it had gone.

"I had to open some presents," she blurted.

"How many?" I asked, as if the number mattered.

"All of them."

Danielle tried to justify herself—"It felt rude not to"—and apologized repeatedly, but I wasn't interested in her explanations. I dropped her off at our house and sat stewing in my car for an hour, half-listening to the Mets game on the radio. When I went inside, she was asleep.

We both woke up early the next morning and didn't speak until Danielle was about to leave for work. She apologized again, wiping tears off her face as she did. By then, I had already forgiven her.

A little more than a month later, Frederick Gustave—Gimpel Ya'acov, after my maternal grandfather—was born. On the morning of Gus's eighth day, he found himself lying atop a pillow on a table in our crowded living room, shrieking. The mohel stood above him admiring his handiwork. "*Now* he looks like a nice Jewish boy," he said. With that, our friends and families started singing.

Epithalamion 2004: A Fable

LOUIS BEGLEY

A young man sits on a bench to the left of steps leading to the college library and feeds pigeons. Because he doesn't like these birds, he is careful to throw the peanuts a good ten feet away from him. He thinks: This is a gratuitous act of kindness. Or perhaps it's expiation for a different gratuitous act, that of his mad mathematician roommate, Otto, committed a week earlier to the nearby asylum that houses more than one member of the American Parnassus. He had been feeding cyanide pellets to pigeons at this very spot, the young man at his side immobile and silent as though he had turned into stone. Soon, the bag that held the peanuts is empty. The young man crumples it and looks for a trash basket. There isn't one to be seen. Instead, he takes in the approach of a tall girl. She wears a red tartan skirt, a beige cardigan sweater, and a necklace of three strands of red beads. Newly shined loafers lead the eye to her ankles and calves. Nice legs. A long braid falls almost to her waist: raven-haired Rapunzel swinging a green book bag! My tire is flat, she says. I borrowed the bicycle and don't know how to work the pump. Can you help?

The young man has no talent for driving in nails, repairing appliances, or dealing with flat tires. Or courting girls, although he likes them a lot. He thinks she is sexy; it's the effect of her assurance, and also of her figure. He allows her to lead him to the bicycle, fiddles diffidently with the pump, and, eureka, he has discovered the way. Once blown up, the tire seems to stay hard. Perhaps it was the tiniest of leaks. They agree that she will have to have it examined by a professional. All at once, the young man feels chagrined. He doesn't know her name, and now she is about to leave. But, at the last minute, her foot already on the pedal, she asks whether he wouldn't like to have a cup of tea in the Square. He has been so gallant. Better yet, would he like to come over for a drink? Here is the address. She lives off campus.

This is, I say, how the story begins, and who will contradict me in matters of my judgment and discretion? Would adding or subtracting this or that detail matter? Time has made layer upon layer of its own indelible revisions. Because I like those names, I will call the girl Mary and the young man Alex.

It helps that she has her own apartment. So does her not being overly difficult, because, for him, it's the first time. Soon sex with her is a necessity. At the same time, he begins to understand the implications of her being so available. How to conceal his jealousy, how to stop her from seeing those other men, how to maintain between Mary and him a balance of power, are questions that nag at Alex without resolution. She torments him by tales of her prior adventures, most often when they are in bed. One evening they are at a party held at a college magazine after a poetry reading. Everyone is drinking heavily the sickeningly sweet punch and gin martinis. At some point, Alex notices that Mary is no longer at his side. He looks for her first in one crowded room and then in another. Flustered, he flips on the light in a back office and finds his startled Eurydice in the lap of a thin-featured man he despises. Vehement words are said. On an impulse, Alex seizes a large, framed group photograph hanging on the wall and breaks it over the fellow's head. The cut is somewhere at the top of the scalp, so that there will be no visible scar, but the blood and shattered glass have made an embarrassing mess. Mary tells Alex that she does not want to see him again. He accepts the banishment, wondering whether the other fellow has taken his place. Although it is almost the end of the academic year, he meets another girl who accepts his advances. The new girl has short hair and, in the dark, wearing a trench coat and a crushed fedora, easily passes for a man. She stays in Alex's room long past the hour when women are required to leave college houses. Sometimes they study, but most of their time together is spent making love. Alex hardly thinks of Mary except to note how much he has learned from her.

During the summer, the new girl's mother falls gravely ill and the girl decides to interrupt her studies to look after her mother in a distant city and keep the father's household. Thus it happens that, when classes resume, Alex is again alone. A friend who is Mary's distant cousin brings her unannounced to dinner with Alex at the house dining room. The cousin jokes broadly that this visit is a liberty he would not have taken before the summer vacation. The meal passes pleasantly, and neither the cousin nor Mary nor Alex finds it strange that Alex should accompany Mary to her apartment. They pick up where they left off. From time to time, Alex asks himself whether he loves Mary. The words he whispers into her ear at night do not answer the question. He knows that they are automatic speech, signaling vacancy of spirit. His need for Mary is beyond doubt, and so is his fear of rupture. In practical terms, however, separation looms near. It is the end of the examination period in Alex's last year at the college, and he has been accepted by a medical school on the West Coast. He would like to report for the draft, but an asthma he has almost forgotten has disqualified him from military service.

In the afternoon of an oppressively hot day in late May, Mary and he walk along the riverbank. She asks whether she shouldn't transfer to the university where he will be enrolling. But you must propose marriage to me first. I think you will like being engaged and being married, she tells him, and offers a sudden, violent caress.

He feels an onset of panic that shuts out the physical pleasure. I am not ready for it, he answers, and hears himself launch into a discourse that he finds both fatuous and discordant. He is talking about his youth, the extreme rigor of medical studies that will not brook the distractions of conjugal existence, and his need for more experience of life.

Then you don't want me, she replies wearily. You had better take me home.

Alex likes to walk fast, and normally Mary is a fast walker as well. The shared tempo of their strides has always exhilarated him. This time she drags her feet along the path. She has taken his arm. Stop waddling, he tells her, let's walk. She shakes her head. He understands that she is in despair and yet resents the dead weight of the body pressing against his side, and the body's unpleasant warmth. The question about love has been answered, and Alex feels almost triumphant. Sullen and thirsty, they reach the Square. He offers a cup of tea, which Mary contemptuously refuses. To cover together the short distance that remains to where she lives is out of the question. They go their separate ways.

Two weeks later, Alex attends his graduation ceremonies. In the Yard, he comes face-to-face with Mary. Her father is a university dignitary, which explains why she is there, although her own graduation is one year away. She holds out her hand for Alex to shake. They speak politely and with great reserve. Then she moves on in the wake of her father. Alex thinks he is seeing her for the last time. Before long she will marry Mr. Right and settle down to raise children in one of those suburbs north of Boston.

For Alex and Mary's good, their story should end now. But it doesn't. Why is that, and why did it not end after the photograph was broken over the head of the man with thin features? Is it because Mary loves Alex? She has rarely permitted him to think so. That he fulfills a need of hers has been, at times, clear to Alex, although he does not understand what she seeks in him. It can't be his lovemaking—she has pointed out its deficiencies pitilessly—and it can't be his looks or anything that might be called social position in the university or elsewhere, because he hasn't any. Perhaps his restless ambition and energy are the magnets. His own desire for her is easy to understand. First and foremost, he is obsessed by her body. The sex with the girl who temporarily replaced Mary was more exciting, and she made him feel that he was a more satisfactory lover. Nonetheless, the power exerted by Mary is far greater. And Mary has opened for him a window on a new world. He was an orphan by the time he was four. The spinster aunt who took him in died while he was still in boarding school; there is no other family; a trust officer in a small-town bank pays his tuition and incidental living expenses out of the remains of his tiny inheritance. At Christmas and on Alex's birthday he sends him a box of maple sugar candy. What a contrast with Mary's family! The parents are at the peak of health and vigor, and cluster with their six children, of whom Mary is the youngest, on the North Shore of Massachusetts. No problem exists, quotidian or loftier, without a solution buttressed by unchallengeable precedent drawn from Shaw founding myths; there is no role for which a Shaw has not adequately been rehearsed; assurance sits on them like Colonel Shaw astride his charger in the Boston Common. Alex is obliged to invent himself continually and to study the ways of strangers: he has no adult models or mentors. But the die is cast. Alex does not abandon his decision to go West because of the chance meeting.

Alex is in the fourth year of medicine, and now that most of his work is in the university hospital with patients, he is certain that he has made the right choice of profession. His resilience stands him in good stead; he must make do with absurdly little sleep, but his serenity is intact, and he hasn't given up books or other interests unrelated to his studies. The brew bubbling in San Francisco's cauldron has much that repels and much that fascinates him. The way he drives the Beetle in which he first crossed the country, it takes him no time at all to get to Haight Ashbury. Some of his classmates are now at Berkeley. He stays in touch with them. Alex still likes girls too much, and he is better at getting them to like him; he credits Mary with having put him through a school for feelings. There is no one girl, however, to whom he feels attached. The camaraderie at the hospital stands in the way of involvements with female interns, of whom there aren't many; he thinks it undignified to make up to nurses; a liaison with one of the women he meets at parties and clubs in San Francisco would call for a commitment of time and attention he tells himself he cannot make. So it's a matter of one-night stands. He has rented a tiny house, minutes away from the hospital, consisting of a bedroom and a room that serves as a combination sitting room and kitchenette, and bordered by a minuscule garden. Not being obliged to live in the dormitory is an indulgence wrested from the bank officer, who still sends him candy and is now approaching retirement.

The telephone wakes him one morning just as he has managed to fall asleep after night duty. It's Mary. She has found him through the alumni office, which is clever of her, she remarks. No one else she knows has the home address at which he can be reached. She will be in San Francisco the following week and would like to see him. He offers to meet her in the city for a drink on an evening when he knows he can get away, but she says she prefers to take a look at him on his own terrain. It's dull, he assures her, but she is not discouraged. She will drive over in a rented car. They have a gin and tonic at his house and then another and she asks whether he doesn't intend to have dinner. Nothing presentable is in his fridge so he takes her to the only restaurant in town that is not a diner; it resembles a Howard Johnson. She drinks more wine than Alex thinks prudent for someone who will be driving back to San Francisco and is, therefore, only half-surprised when she asks

177

whether she can sleep over. In the trunk of her car is an overnight bag. The surprise comes later, after they have necked extensively on the sitting room couch: she announces that she will not sleep with him. Exasperated, he considers throwing her out or, more accurately, proposing to drive her over to the motel where students' parents usually stay. But he has to get up early the next morning and wants to avoid a drunken argument. Besides, he no longer feels aroused. He puts sheets and a blanket on the couch, gives her the first turn in the bathroom, and goes to sleep in his bedroom with the door shut. He doesn't know at what time of the night she slips under his covers.

The overnight bag is more capacious than it at first appeared. Mary stays a week; then, after a quick trip alone to San Francisco, returns with more clothes and other necessaries. She has not met the right man, although one or two had seemed to hold promise; and she didn't go to graduate school to pursue her interest in American colonial history. Instead she has traveled through Italy, staying at I Tatti and then at the American Academy in Rome, whose director was best man at her parents' wedding. Then she fell sick, which complicated everything. Alex's questions—he is learning the art of patient interviews—bring to light the nature of the illness: it's what some would call a nervous breakdown, followed by a stay in a establishment renowned for Freudian orthodoxy. She tells Alex that to be with him she has interrupted further treatment, which is analysis in Boston. Mary stops short of hinting that the way she and Alex parted on the riverbank pushed her over the line, but he does not doubt that his actions have been enshrined in the etiology of her troubles. Fortunately, a list of traumas far more arcane long predate that afternoon. They cast a harsh light on the Shaw myths.

The final-examination season begins, and Alex works night and day, especially hard because hospital duties are not reduced to give students time to study. Mary comes and goes between Palo Alto and

San Francisco. When she returns from her consultations with the doctor in Boston, Alex diagnoses her mood as serene. He plans to work at the university hospital until one of the internships he has applied for comes through; although he is at the top of the class, and there is a strong desire to keep him as an intern right where he is, the general view is that his career will benefit from a change of scene. When the results of the examinations are announced, Alex wishes that at least his aunt were still alive so he could tell her. Instead, he tells Mary. They drink champagne and afterward make love. Dinner can wait. Alex thinks that perhaps she now loves him. But what does he mean by that word? He has begun to understand how Mary's state of drift, and her pursuit of him, link with whatever it is that she and the analyst in Boston are exploring. In moments of gloom, she tells him that she is sick. But the training Alex has received inclines him to a skeptical view. She is a rich girl, with a rich girl's fashionable affliction.

The remaining weeks in Palo Alto are punctuated by Mary's quick trips to Boston. This is the time of year when the heat in northern California can be oppressive. When Mary is there, and Alex has time off, they drive to Pebble Beach and dive into the frigid waves. One day, when Mary is in Boston, the news comes by phone to the hospital: he has been offered an internship in a great hospital in New York City. His heart had been set on it. He calls Mary at the number she has given him. A man answers. Alex resists the sudden impulse to hang up and leaves his name. There will be no champagne that evening, but on the way home from the hospital he sends a telegram to the bank trust officer. The old fellow will be glad, even if he cannot measure the importance of Alex's achievement. The next day, Mary reaches Alex, also at the hospital. It should have been easy enough to find him at home during the night, is the thought that crosses his mind as he takes the call at the nurses' station. Where are you staying? he asks her. With a friend. He leaves it at that and whispers, Guess what, it's New York. He

179

doesn't want anyone to hear him brag. Mary gasps and tells him she is catching the next plane.

Before long, the issue is joined. Alex's books, a good half of them acquired while he was at college and a few that had belonged to his parents or his aunt, and his collection of LPs, furnish the occasion. Mary hears him arrange to ship them to the dormitory that the hospital in New York maintains for interns and breaks out in rage. You are really doing it, she taunts. You have finally figured out how to get rid of me. Even if you must live in a cubicle to do it. There is no arguing with her when she is like that: it isn't as if she didn't know that he can't afford to live in a New York hotel while he looks for an apartment. Or that an apartment near the hospital that fits his budget probably doesn't exist. By nightfall, she is calm, but it's a calm that he has learned to distrust. You have to decide, she tells him. Are you going to look after me? That's the question. I don't want to hear another word about love. He thinks he is living through a replay of the scene on the riverbank four years ago. All the reasons why he cannot undertake a larger commitment are known, they have been rehearsed ad nauseam: his youth and poverty, the arduous program of work that he has undertaken, her desire for a normal married life just like everybody else's. Only this time the scene ends differently. Alex will not run the risk of losing Mary. The offer of marriage is duly made and accepted.

Some days later, they make preparations to spend the Labor Day weekend on the North Shore with Mary's parents and the rest of the tribe. Alex pieces together some remarks she makes, and it becomes clear that the male friend who answered the telephone when she was last in Boston is the odious man with narrow features. How could you have done that? he asks. The light-headedness he is experiencing is like the state one of his professors has described as sometimes preceding a stroke. Why shouldn't I have? she replies. I didn't stay at his apartment to fuck him; I can do that anytime. They go to bed late, but he is awake just before dawn. Careful not to disturb her sleep, he goes out into the little garden. What ails Mary is not just an heiress's pastime. He sees a life of stony misery stretching before them. This is the moment to break the engagement, but there is no going back. He has given his word.

They are married a short time later at a hunt club near the place where Mary's parents' live. Alex asks his old roommate Otto to be the best man. Electroshock and a maintenance diet of pills have had the desired effect: Otto is in graduate school, close to a doctorate in theoretical physics. His long hair is greasy, he still suffers from acne, but the cutaway he has borrowed from his father has an elegance about it that mutes the Shaws' disapproval.

When did the bad fairy mutter the curse that hangs over them?

It does not take long for the pattern of Alex and Mary's married life to be set. During the first year, sex with her transports him to the ultimate limits of pleasure. Early in the following year, Mary becomes inconsolable: she has gone into mourning. The ministrations of the short, brusque man ensconced in a basement apartment of an East Side brownstone bring only momentary improvement, and yet they are indispensable. On occasion, the underground man summons Alex to his office, asks a question or two, drums his fingers on the desk, and dismisses him. Alex hates him, as he hates every man who approaches Mary. Except for her dreadful sadness, Alex and Mary live like mommy and daddy— like Mary's mommy and daddy, to be more precise, because neither the apartment on the East River, nor its renovation, nor the nice Irish maid, and certainly not the services of the underground man could conceivably be paid for by Alex. What is to be done for her? The answer appears to Alex in a moment of nocturnal rapture. These have become rare; on many nights Alex must be at the hospital, and when he is at home, Mary as often as not bars the road to her bed. He whispers, Let's make a child! It takes no time at all for Mary to conceive. They call the little girl

181

Hope, after Mary's Shaw grandmother. The maternal grand-mother's name is Patience: Alex balks at that suggestion.

When it comes to the choice of continuing his training as a resident, Alex can have his pick of hospitals and departments. He would not object to moving to Boston, where the meager salary would go further. But Mary hisses and spits like a cornered cat. Haven't you understood yet, she asks, that they broke me there? The truth is that he doesn't understand certain reinterpretations of Mary's history. No matter; he has decided he will be a neurologist, the greatest intellectual challenges are to be found there. The head of the department at his hospital, a world-famous authority on brainwashing, wants to take Alex under his wing. Alex likes the great man. He thinks of him as Mr. 1984, but that is not a joke that he shares with Mary. He accepts the offer.

The truth is that Alex and Mary share few jokes and fewer moments of gaiety. Hope is a lovely baby, but Mary is an anxious and unhappy mother. Astonishingly, Alex's choice of residency provokes a new row over money. Mary's oldest brother, a lantern-jawed lawyer, habitually got up in navy blue pinstripes cut for him by a gnome in the eaves of Brooks Bros. to fit his lanky and stooped frame, is a partner in a New York firm that looks after trusts of the very rich. He invites Alex to his office and lays it on the line. What business have you, he asks, to choose a specialty that won't lead to your making a decent living? We think you've had a good free ride and it's about time you started paying for your household. Alex protests, But I do, I pay over every cent of my salary and everything I have besides. A drop in the bucket, replies the brother; it won't do. Alex is puzzled. He asks what the brother thinks he should do. Put your career on a different track, is the answer. It turns out that, at Mary's behest, the brother has consulted a medical friend or two and learned that there is no pot of gold in neurology. Only pediatricians earn less. I see, says Alex, you think I should do abortions. The brother doesn't break a sweat. Obstetrics, he remarks, could indeed be more rewarding, but that is for you to decide. For the time being, since you can't meet your commitments to your family, a program of borrowing is in order. There will be a promissory note, payable to Mary in the amount she has expended, for you to sign at the end of every month. I will make the notes fall due in seven years' time or earlier, if you and Mary should separate. Between you and me, adds the brother, I don't think these notes will be worth the paper they're written on. But for Mary it's a matter of principle.

So that is what they do. Alex signs the notes as they are presented and hands them over to Mary, who accepts these pieces of paper without comment other than on the amount of money she is spending and how much he now owes her. Alex agrees that they are spending a lot: there are now nannies in addition to the maid, and soon there will be nursery school as well.

Years pass. Richard Nixon is in the White House and America is more than ever mired in Southeast Asia. Alex has joined the practice of the great neurologist on Park Avenue, he is an assistant professor at the hospital, he publishes articles in scientific periodicals that arouse enough interest to be mentioned in leading dailies and some of the general-interest magazines. Hope is at the most elegant of the East Side girls' schools, but the demands of its academic program—modest, in Alex's opinion—may not be matched by her development. Moreover, the school's notions of deportment, and those of the parents of Hope's classmates, clash with Mary's current views. These have taken on a deep Woodstock coloration. While the underground man has not yet lifted the lead cloak that weighs on Mary, his guidance is invaluable and wide-ranging. His twin boys attend a progressive place of learning newly established in a mansion off Fifth Avenue; that is where Hope transfers. Tie-dyed long skirts and T-shirts replace the school uniform; there is no more talk of Miss Proper's dancing class. The load of debt to Mary is

Alex's lead cloak. He has begun to pay it down and no longer needs to borrow from Mary for current expenses, especially as she has at last agreed to pay the bills of the underground man from her own pocket. But the maturity of those notes is approaching fast, and Alex doesn't expect any forbearance. There is nothing of the flower child about Mary when it comes to money. Indeed, Alex doesn't believe that she wishes him well. He sleeps now on a daybed in the room that is called his study. When he lies awake at night, he tries to imagine what it will be like to grow old, to pass the rest of his life, at the side of a woman who is his enemy. To be fair, he probes his own feelings. What he discovers makes him ashamed.

Alex continues to like women more than he thinks he should. He takes note of those who find him attractive, not a few of Mary's own friends among them. Casual affairs, wife-switching, and group gropes in clubs one hears of on the West Side have come into vogue in Alex and Mary's milieu. But Alex's rigorous schedule, and the combined surveillance of his receptionist, the duty nurses at the hospital, and the answering service, make the logistics of adultery unmanageable, except during the month when Mary is away. He doesn't take advantage of that opportunity, perhaps because those women who seem to find him attractive are also out of town, perhaps because he is not willing to be an accomplice to destroying the marriage bond. Alex's jealousy has not abated, but he is so busy with the hospital and his practice that the opacity of Mary's daily life, when he asks himself whether he has rivals, is nearly total. The underground man? The ponytailed artistes who have tea or cocktails in his and Mary's apartment and flee, leaving a faint wake of cannabis smoke, if by chance he appears? Old pals on the North Shore when she spends August there with Hope while the underground man rests from his labors in the pine woods of Cape Cod? These questions go unanswered, unless her not wanting him is all the answer he needs. One fact is clear: separation and divorce are recurring subjects of Mary's tirades. She tells Alex that his dependence on her, and his egotism and passion for control, are a blight. She wants him to leave the house and leave the marriage. When he pleads with her to relent and promises to change, she tells him it's too late, she doesn't trust him. Alex peers into the stony desert stretching ahead of him and capitulates. He knows that Hope is a nervous child. His departure may make her life calmer, if not better. When he speaks to the child about the fun they will have once he has an apartment of his own and they can go on their private expeditions and vacations, she looks at him coolly and says, I know you and Mommy are getting divorced. Then she clams up.

Alex is in frequent touch with Otto, who has veered from graduate studies to managing a café in the East Village, where poets read their works late into the night, often to the accompaniment of music, and where certain drugs may be purchased. The evening Alex moves from the apartment in which he has lived with Mary into a residential hotel, he calls Otto, thinking he might go downtown to see him. There is no answer. Alex checks the number and tries again without success. He finds the explanation the next day in the metropolitan section of the newspaper. The owner of a village hangout was found dead by the cleaning crew, his throat cut. An old photograph of Otto accompanies the article.

Mary's divorce lawyer is the man with thin features. Alex sees him for the first time since college in his own lawyer's office, where he signs the documents that put him and Mary asunder. The fellow is as odious as ever and has taken to wearing a derby. Quite possibly, he has grown more sententious. We all commit mistakes, he says, the great wisdom is not to remain chained to them. Alex's suspicions about the use to which Mary put his hospitality in Boston are intensified. Afterward Alex's own lawyer says to him, someday you will be grateful to her. You are free to start a new life now. In Alex's opinion, these observations are also sententious and grossly impertinent.

*   *   *

185

It is the year of the capture of Saddam Hussein.

Soon after Alex and she parted, Mary married the man with thin features and a derby hat, bore him two children, and then divorced and remarried. The current husband is the underground man, not the first in his profession to find solace with a patient. Hope brings Alex occasional news of her mother. They are better friends, Hope and her father, now that she is a grown woman. He wishes that she could detach herself from the fellow she lives with, whose commitment to his wife appears to trump whatever feelings he has for Hope.

And Alex? Mary's harsh view of him was not far off the mark. I saw little but loneliness and disappointments ahead of him. The turbulence and aridity of his existence after the divorce confirmed the judgment of the cards. Then a smiling lady, of beauty and bearing so regal that he and everyone around him wondered whether she was a princess in disguise, embraced Alex and broke the spell. She did not change him from a frog back into what he had been before; her charm was stronger. She transformed him into a new man, appeased and trusting. The smiling lady and Alex have lived happily ever after.

The Plan

DAVID OWEN

My own wedding was the first one I ever saw, except on TV or in a movie. Same for my wife. You can tell from the photographs that we didn't know what was going on: we look stricken. This was in 1978. I was twenty-three and Ann was twenty-one, and no one we knew was even thinking about getting married. We had just graduated from college—where we had met, a year and a half earlier, while using butter knives to scrape dried vomit from the floor of the basement of the *Harvard Lampoon*. My sister visited a couple of weeks later and told me, "If you don't marry her, you won't marry anyone." Ann and I lived together that summer, along with six other undergraduates, in a house that the *Lampoon* had rented from Harvey Cox, a professor in the Divinity School and the author of an unlikely hippie-era bestseller called *The Secular City*. The most striking thing about the house (aside from the fact that Cox had consented to rent it to eight irresponsible adolescents) was that none of the rooms contained a lamp bright enough for comfortable reading. The eight of us spent the summer bickering, flooding the basement with sewage, making a doll's-head-and-cigarette-butt construction we called Baby Lenore, betting on the greyhounds at Wonderland, mourning the death of Elvis Presley, having hangovers, preparing inedible meals, failing to respect the property of others, and during the last few days of August, writing *The Harvard Lampoon's Big Book of College Life,* which would later fail to earn back a five-thousand-dollar advance. At some point during the summer, Ann and I decided to get married. To the best of my recollection, neither of us proposed per se.

Somehow, I guess, we had known all along. Practically our first conversation had concerned the desirability of emulating the legendary *New Yorker* writer E. B. White by living on a farm in New England and being famous writers—exactly what we have ended up doing, minus the farm and the fame. The stepfather of my best friend warned me that we were crazy to get married so young, and I lied to him by telling him we knew what we were doing. My future uncle-in-law warned me about the recklessness of moving to New York City without securing real jobs first, as we were preparing to do, and I lied to him too. I don't remember feeling particularly anxious, at that point, about how we would get by. I must have figured that things would probably work out somehow, as they generally had before.

There's a lot to be said for acting impetuously when you're young. Clueless people are more likely to be smart by accident than on purpose, so why not roll the dice? Having a deeper understanding of adult responsibilities could only have made us less likely to do what turned out to be the right thing. If people in their early twenties knew as much about life as people in their forties and fifties and sixties do, they'd be paralyzed. Either that, or they'd all end up in law school.

Ann and I did have a few ideas about what marriage would entail—most of them wrong, it turned out. Ann thought married women didn't wear jeans or listen to records, so she almost left those things behind when we loaded our possessions into a rented Ryder truck before moving to the city. I thought husbands wore big dark shoes with laces, so I bought two pairs. I wore the black ones at the wedding—a friend laughed when he saw them, and called them "night watchman shoes"—and I never wore the brown ones after the day I tried them on. Gradually, over years, both pairs acquired a thick coating of closet dust while curling into the shape of elf shoes. When we moved to the country, not quite twenty years ago, I threw them away.

During most of the seven years we lived in New York, Ann and I were the only people our age we knew who were married. As a result, we owned a lot of stuff that our friends didn't, such as guest towels, silverware made of silver, and three woks. There was always a box of Kleenex in our bathroom—a novelty in our circle. When single male friends came over for dinner, they ate mind-boggling quantities of whatever Ann had cooked, the only family-type meal they'd encountered since the last time they'd visited. Some of our single friends seemed almost like characters in sitcoms; they would drop by unannounced at odd hours, happy to sprawl on our couch drinking beer and watching *Family Feud,* lonesome for domesticity.

My first job, as a fact-checker for a weekly magazine, paid $165 a week. Even before taxes, that barely covered the rent on our apartment. At one point, I decided that everything would be okay if I could just borrow a thousand dollars, so I spent part of one lunch hour pleading with a loan officer at a big bank near Grand Central Station. He turned me down, as he should have. There was some sort of milk strike in the city in late 1978 or early 1979—of dairy workers? of milk truck drivers?—and on my own initiative I wrote a brief article humorously describing my efforts to rent a cow. The editor published it but decided it merited no compensation beyond my salary. Soon after that, I quit, despite not knowing what I might do next. Ann, meanwhile, had gone to work, as a volunteer dog walker for an obscure humane organization (a form of employment appropriate for a wife, she felt then).

Ann later found paying jobs, as a writer and as an editor. And I, after weeks of anxious unemployment, persuaded a publisher to let me spend a semester pretending to be a high school student, then write a book about my experience. Each weekday for four months, I commuted by train between Manhattan and a large public high school near Bridgeport, Connecticut, where I studied algebra, read *Beowulf,* went to gym class, and hung out with directionless seventeen-year-olds, none of whom knew I was an impostor. That was a pretty good idea for a book, I think, although I wonder, now, about my real motivation. Had a few months of marriage made me subconsciously long to return to a premarital form of existence? Ann apparently had similar doubts. Chatting with my mother during some early visit, she began a thought, "When David goes . . ."—a slip that indicated she too had permitted herself to imagine the likely bliss of spouselessness.

Anyway, we got past all that. Marrying young, it turns out, has numerous practical advantages. For one thing, the universe of bothersome ex-boyfriends and ex-girlfriends is considerably smaller. For another thing, you gradually become inured to the developing eccentricities of your mate rather than having them thrust upon you full-blown and all at once. A good friend of mine postponed marriage until he was nearly forty, by which time he had evolved so many stubborn quirks that sharing a roof with him has required major, unsettling compromises from his bride and from himself. Ann and I, in contrast, essentially grew up together and have therefore been able to acquire independent interests the way siblings do, without weakening the underlying bond. If I had been a golf nut and power-tool obsessive when we met, or if Ann had already taken up ice hockey and Sunday-school teaching, we might not have made it to a first date. One of my golf buddies, who is in his early fifties, is about to remarry after more than a decade of living alone. The main order of business for him and his fiancé has been deciding which parts of both lives will have to be chucked.

By the time our friends were beginning to get married, Ann and I had decided to have children. Ann was twenty-six when she got pregnant, and I was twenty-eight—ancient by the standards of the world, but shockingly young among the people we knew. Buying baby equipment was deeply satisfying, like discovering a previously unsuspected continent of consumption. And because almost all our friends were childless, we got to make our purchases without having to listen to much advice.

When our daughter was born, I was working at home as a freelance writer, and Ann was working as an editor at a book publishing company. We both wanted to keep our jobs, and we didn't want (and couldn't afford) to hire a nanny, so we devised an equitable scheme for dividing child-care responsibilities between us: I looked after our daughter and did the cooking while Ann was at work on Mondays, Tuesdays, Thursdays, and Fridays, and Ann was in charge after work, on weekends, and on Wednesdays (when her employer allowed her to "work at home"). I had been concerned, before our daughter was born, that becoming a father would reduce my already marginal productivity as a writer; instead, it did the opposite. Preparenthood, my daily routine had consisted of getting up at ten or eleven, reading every word in the *New York Times* while drinking many cups of coffee and smoking five cigarettes (my self-imposed daily allotment), airing the apartment to get rid of the visible smoke, mining the refrigerator, making telephone calls, doing unnecessary errands, and—beginning around four—writing listlessly for a couple of hours before knocking off for cocktails and an evening of leisure. Now I rose when my daughter did, worked feverishly when she napped and when Ann was on duty, didn't smoke, and somehow doubled my income despite having cut my potential work time by more than half. I also discovered that I liked hanging around with a baby, that diapers didn't bother me a bit, and that I enjoyed being fussed over by strange women when we went shopping or took the dog for a walk.

Summarized in this way, Ann's and my system sounds like the product of a carefully worked-out theory of childrearing, but it was actually something we contrived on the fly, shortly before the end of Ann's four-month maternity leave. During the pregnancy, we—like

191

most first-time parents—had focused mainly on the birth itself, viewing it as the scary culmination of a nine-month adventure rather than as the threshold of an utterly transformed life. The real duties of parenthood became evident to us only as we began to exercise them. Our scheme for dividing the week started as a plausible solution to a problem we hadn't fully foreseen. Later, though, it would grow into something bigger.

When our daughter was almost a year old, Ann and I decided that the time had finally come for us to make our E. B. White move. Our apartment seemed impossibly cramped, and our daughter was walking, and we yearned for a yard. One Wednesday, while Ann and the baby stayed home, I rented a car from Rent-a-Wreck and drove alone to a small Connecticut town a little more than two hours north of the city—a town that neither Ann nor I had ever visited but that seemed about the right distance away. A real estate agent showed me a house that was more or less in what I had told her was our price range. I said the house seemed too small. She showed me a second house, which was considerably larger. It was two hundred years old, and between 1943 and 1969 it had served as a dormitory for a boys' boarding school, and in 1970 it had been cut in two and moved on the back of a truck to its present location. I told the real estate agent that it seemed big enough, and that I would take it. She was flabbergasted. She said, "Don't you think your wife ought to see it first?" I said, "Oh, I'm sure she'll like it."

Ann didn't like it, actually, when she saw it for the first time, a few weeks later. (I had had trouble finding it again, after also having had trouble finding the town.) The rooms were filled with horrible wallpaper, the garage was falling down, and an occupied apartment was on the third floor, among other concerns. Nevertheless, looking for another house struck both of us as an awful nuisance. Finding this house had taken me almost an entire morning; what was I supposed to do, rent another car? That night, after a brief, gloomy discussion, we decided, in effect, to roll the dice with our lives once again.

Nearly twenty years later, we're still in the same house—although the wallpaper, the old garage, and the apartment are gone, among a great many other changes. Little by little, in fact, we have remodeled nearly every inch, proceeding whenever we were in funds and had forgotten how irritating the previous project had been. Home improvement is cumulative and reciprocal: changing our house, mostly by trial and error, has changed us too. Today, I feel almost as though the place had been built to our specifications, although if you had handed me a blank check on the day we moved in, I wouldn't have known what to do with it.

Everything else worked out too, eventually. We didn't know anyone in town when we arrived, but the lawyer who handled our closing had a daughter the same age as our daughter, and I ran into the lawyer's wife at the grocery store a few days later and she invited us to join her playgroup. The kids in that playgroup became our daughter's friends, and their parents became our friends. The kids are all in college now, but their parents are still the people Ann goes to church with, the people I play golf with, the people we both will grow old with. As with our decision to get married in the first place, taking a witless chance on where to live turned out to be pretty shrewd—and why not? If you don't know what you're doing, simply gathering more facts is unlikely to improve the outcome. The critical step in a journey is seldom the first one. Maybe we would have found a better life if we had looked another month or another year or another decade. Or maybe not.

Ann had to quit her editing job when we moved to the country, and she too became a freelance writer. With both of us now working at home, we were able to refine our child-care system. We decided to alternate getting up with our daughter—me today, you tomorrow—and to change shifts at ten. The parent who took over at ten also gave her lunch and put her down for her nap, at one. (That nap, which almost always lasted two hours, was the foundation of our family economy: a dependable block of work time in the middle of the day.) The first-shift parent got her up from her nap and made dinner; we switched again after dinner, for bath and books and bedtime. When our son was born, two and a half years after we moved in, we modified the schedule again several times, eventually ending up with a system in which one parent was on duty with both kids until one in the afternoon, the other was on duty from one until dinner, and each parent took one child from the end of dinner until bed. This may have spoiled our kids to some extent: just as one parent's interest in playing Timothy the Horse was beginning to flag, a fresh parent materialized to take over. But because we divided the load, we felt far less overwhelmed than full-time single caregivers often do.

Friends and relatives teased us for timing our shifts to the minute, and for operating what was essentially a private secondary market in child-care debt. (If one parent had to miss a shift or go out of town for some reason—always arranged and agreed to well in advance—the other parent accumulated child-care credit, which we tracked on paper and which the holder was then able to spend.) What our friends didn't understand about our system was that its rigidity was liberating rather than oppressive. Because Ann knew that I was getting up with the kids, she could sleep in with a free conscience; because I knew that she would take over at the stroke of ten, I could confidently schedule an activity of my own for 10:01. What's more, if I decided to play golf during time when I was off duty, I knew that I could do it without having to slink out of the house, even if one of the children was crying. The parent on duty was the parent on duty.

When other parents we knew tried to share child-care responsibilities without defining them first—on a weekend, maybe, or during a vacation—they often fell into passive-aggressive struggles that left neither parent fully engaged or fully free and gave their children numerous opportunities to exploit the guilt-ridden bafflement of both. Because our system was inflexible, it was never in doubt. When you were on, you were on; when you were off, you were blameless. It was something our kids could depend on too. They even internalized it and instinctively knew, for example, which side of our bed to come to in the middle of the night if they'd had a bad dream, based on who had given them their bath. They also knew that the off-duty parent was not available for an appeal or a second opinion if they disagreed with a ruling handed down by the on-duty parent. Certain things I alone allowed the kids to do, and certain things Ann alone allowed the kids to do; they knew to wait.

Ann's and my system—combined, of course, with the lucky accident that we both had jobs we could do at home, piecemeal, at odd hours—meant that we got to share our children's childhoods in a way that most couples can't. It was the biggest undertaking of our lives, and we did it together, even though we did it mostly in nonoverlapping shifts. That was good for our kids, I hope; it was definitely good for us. In fact, it became the foundation of our marriage—maybe even the purpose of our marriage. That wasn't what we'd intended when we'd started out. And it was nothing we could have anticipated back in college, when we decided, what the hell, to spend the rest of our lives together. But you can't plan everything.

The Waiting Game

CHIP BROWN

Among the earliest revelations of my married life was that I married late, or what would be called late anywhere but New York, and even in New York where the social pressure to settle down and breed is offset by the premium on getting somewhere in your profession, forty-three is pushing it. This dour news was delivered by my future mother-in-law the first time we met in the fall of 1995. We were having an inspect-the-new-fiancé lunch at a restaurant in the basement of a department store off Madison Avenue. Kate's mom, elegantly dressed in an Armani jacket, elicited my job history and family background, graciously holding neither of them against me. And then, like a skilled detective, she pounced. "How come you haven't been snapped up?" she said. Translated, that would be: *Christ, you're forty-three years old, you've never been married, what the hell is wrong with you?*

Oh, where to begin? Had it been some other occasion I might have risked a joke: the new fiancé didn't get snapped up because his electroconvulsive therapy took longer than expected, or something. In truth I was damp with anxiety and too paralyzed by the question to laugh it off. Some departures from standard practice are rewarded as freethinking innovations, but to delay marriage past a certain point is to call down a torrent of speculation about what psychical blight might be hindering you from committing to one person, getting a mortgage, having kids, buying apple juice by the gallon, learning the names of the Teletubbies, and generally doing what you can to act like a responsible monogamous adult, thereby contributing to the progress and glory of civilization.

Of course the double edge in my mother-in-law's question about why I hadn't gotten married in years past was why I should suddenly want to do so now, and to her daughter of all people. Why enmesh Kate in some out-of-character marriage scheme? Someone who had obviously taken pains to build a history of shirked responsibilities and discarded passions ought to have a clear idea why he wanted to veer off in a new direction. What were my *reasons*?

I could see Kate was curious too. But as coils of shopgirl perfume spiraled down through the open ceiling, I sat dumbly on the banquette thinking I would never find a way to explain what seemed an ineffably mysterious intuition. Somewhere in the silence a breadstick snapped. Hoping to regain the use of my larynx, I sipped some water, but it went down the wrong way and I promptly started to drown. It took forever for the choking and hacking to subside, but when it was over, I found myself saying that I had waited a long time to marry *because a long time was what it had taken to find Kate*. The desperate sentiment seemed to make Kate happy and to put her mom at ease too, and the conversation moved on to wedding dates and caterers.

Now we are approaching our eighth anniversary. We have a mortgage, and a son. We oversee an apple juice storage facility with Laa-Laa and Tinky Winky. Like all couples we also have a creation myth, the story of how we met and chose to marry. The basic facts of *where* and *when* don't change. They are immutable. They can, however, be stretched for theatrical effect, and they often are, at my expense, alas.

Kate quickly discovered it was so hilarious to describe in gratuitously vivid detail how her clueless husband woke up one day and

197

realized he had neglected to get married. So he ran down to the Condé Nast building—also off Madison Avenue at that time—and he combed the directory of the women's magazines that were then housed one to a floor and were well-known to be teeming with witty and stylish sylphs who lunched alone on Caesar salads and didn't get asked out much because they always had to stay late at the office writing perky captions. And because the staff often embodied the editorial aesthetic of each magazine, Kate's husband-to-be, a geriatric freelance writer, was able to make some canny snap judgments about the best floor to rake for a wife. *Glamour?* Too down-market. *Self?* Too narcissistic. *Modern Bride?* Too much tulle. *Vogue?* Bingo! And there he was in his goofy purple gloves outside her office door, gaping at her Azzedine Alaia suit and eavesdropping reverently as she cursed on the phone in French. When she hung up, he asked if she wanted to play tennis or something; it was January with over-the-knee snow on the courts in Central Park.

As I say, the *where* and *when* are matters of fact, easy to ascertain. It's the *why* of the creation story that seems elusive, in some ways almost incommunicable. I accept that what Kate saw in me, why she wanted to be my wife, is and will always be an enigma beyond even the scope of an all-knowing God. (She likes to say I disabled her better judgment by plying her with Château Palmer and proposing in the romance-soaked atmosphere of Paris.) But it's one thing not to fully understand her motives, and another not to fully understand my own. What was it about her that claimed my heart? That filled me with the resolve to break old patterns? Where did the impetus to change come from? It can't be explained by willowy beauty, Alaia suits, and the ability to curse French, provocative as they are. I guess what I'm asking ultimately is, Where does love come from, and what precipitates these mysterious intuitions that lead us to it?

It's dreadfully embarrassing to open the journal I kept in those days and find a spineless dear-diary character yearning for fulfill-ment: *What I want is to fall in love, love understood not as an act of will but as a stroke of fortune, a transpersonal state one is lucky enough to stumble into like a Star Trek character snatched up by a subspace distortion.*

Maybe, on second thought, willowy beauty and Alaia suits were more provocative than I realized, especially in conjunction with the sea light in Kate's eyes, and the marvelous swoop in her voice when she said "Quelle horreur!" or when she rebuffed an obtrusively personal question with an incredulous "Excuse me?" And there was also that she was afraid of swans and once spent a day on a couch watching MTV after a bad breakup, and when we started e-mailing each other, she signed her messages "love."

There were—there are—a thousand reasons. And yet none seem especially conclusive or sharply defined. It's as if it is their nature to change as the nature of the marriage changes. This protean quality of the creation story makes it seem like a painting whose hidden depths and meanings are only revealed over time. I must have had some inkling of the deeper reasons when I got married, despite being unable to articulate them under pressure. But even now they remain tantalizingly beyond my grasp, hinted at in the structure of our marriage, its unspoken rules, its unique and wordless language.

At the beginning, the creation story is essentially a hypothesis without data. When the data starts coming in, you starting sub-stantiating your theories or junking them. Early on I wondered (quietly to myself), if Kate and I were just puppets of biology and timing. The age paradigm says if you marry young, you are probably being propelled by hormones and perhaps naïve romantic idealism. If you marry late, in all likelihood you are being lashed by intimations of mortality. Past a certain age, forty-three probably, marriage has to be considered less a profound tribal rite than a game of musical chairs. You marry the person you're sitting next to when the music stops. In other words, what's love got to do with it?

The music stops and you hightail it over to the Condé Nast building.

Has the data discredited this scenario? I would be rushing to say yes, but it's foolish to discount the imperatives of the body. It's likely love has less to do with our romantic self-conceptions than with the chemistry of instinctual behavior, the grammar of hormones, or, giving culture its place, the biologically coercive effects of red wine, peer pressure, and chocolate. Along these lines, my inability to comprehend my own motives and report them to my mother-in-law, my chronic feeling of being haunted by reasons just out of reach, cast doubt on the idea that I'm exerting meaningful control over my fate or am really in charge of all that much. Is there any psychological illusion more diabolical than this conceit of presidential agency? Recall the cheerful paradox of Hume's fork as defined in the *Oxford Dictionary of Philosophy*: "Either our actions are determined, in which case we are not responsible for them, or they are the result of random events, in which case we are also not responsible for them." Whatever we think, or how we live, life mostly works in us, not through us, and we have precious little to say about its terms—in fact almost nothing to say about the terms of love, and only a little bit more about the terms of marriage.

I remember the sense of a larger force at work when my younger brother, Toby, got married at age twenty-five. Waiting for the ceremony to begin on the altar of an Episcopal church in Connecticut, he seemed relaxed, laughing when the young organist wove the theme from *The Flintstones* into the prelude. But when Anne appeared at the end of the aisle, he began to tremble. Maybe it was the rustle of the organ, but the sound in the church was like the clamor of surf, as if we were all standing by the ocean or inside a giant shell. You could feel the presence of the life force shuddering in its traces, impatient to get the ceremony out of the way so the real work of minting fresh DNA could begin. It seemed at that moment, free will notwithstanding, my brother and his wife were but the means to an end, the instruments of their genes, clapped together by a design much more consequential than their personalities, or their ostensible reasons for getting married. The machinery of life proceeds independently of vows.

When you marry late, you flatter yourself that you can coolly appraise the compulsions of hormones and genes. You are tempted to indulge the dangerous conceit that your wise old head is impervious to the gods of biochemistry. I would have sworn on the eve of my wedding that because I had had the luxury of biding my time about marriage, I was acting more judiciously than someone younger—that indeed my decision to tie the knot marked the end of a protracted adolescence.

Only a true subspace distortion could have produced that theory. For starters I had bided my time almost down to nothing and felt that at forty-three, my eligibility was waning faster than a shelf of unrefrigerated yogurt. I was lingering around the Condé Nast building with a sense of urgency, not leisure. And as for that supposed postadolescent maturity, it took only a couple of married fights to dash that vanity. *Judicious* is the last word for the way the venomous subtext of marital grievance can trigger infantile regression in otherwise mentally well-adjusted adults and turn a minor skirmish into Armageddon.

One of Kate's and my most dramatic fights made me wonder whether marriage signals not the demise of adolescence but perhaps its perverse triumph. The battle occurred on the Long Island Expressway over whether we had missed the exit to the Whitestone Bridge. I have blocked the underlying issues—probably something to do with where the marriage was going and who was doing the emotional driving and who just was along for the ride—but it ended with denunciations and promises that divorce lawyers would be summoned first thing Monday.

The onset of hostilities is so common to most marriages that it

201

delineates the start of the posthoneymoon phase, which as I remember from an article in the online edition of *Ladies' Home Journal* is called "The What Have I Done?" phase. (It could as easily be called the "Trying to Understand My Spouse, I Turn Desperately to Articles by Lame Academics in *Ladies' Home Journal*" phase.) In any case, the bottom line is that people who marry late enjoy no special exemption from the juvenile insanity of marital conflict. What we are actually doing is adding the delusion of levelheaded maturity to the blindness of hormone-addled youth. If the forces that generate a marriage are not necessarily the ones that sustain it, they do seem to have a common source. By some grace, Kate and I made it over the Whitestone Bridge without a wreck, and now we read the creation story of what induced us to marry in light of what keeps us together.

These years later I daresay that I have seen some veils lifted from the inscrutable face of Kate's interest in me. Last winter, having gone to bed around one A.M., I woke up a couple of hours later and couldn't get back to sleep. I got up. Our son, Oliver, was soundly sawing zees in the next room. After checking on him, I made some tea in the kitchen and turned on the computer. I read some *Ladies' Home Journal* articles online. Finally around six thirty, I climbed back in bed and fell asleep. Just as I was getting launched on a REM period, I felt someone shaking my shoulder. A dream? No, my wife, my bride, light of my waking life, but now, inexplicably, the scourge of my sleep. When I opened my eyes, she was holding a bottle of self-tanning lotion.

"I need you to help me put self-tanning lotion on my back," she said.

Groggy, bewildered, irritated, amazed, I flashed on novelist Ward Just's observation that what keeps marriages together is "civility, compromise, and the suppression of rage." Beyond exasperation was flabbergasted awe at the spectacle of her chutzpah.

And then I saw another facet of that elusive *why*: a rationale of marriage tied to the ways in which we were willing to indulge one another. *Hey, at least she needs me. If I get up and help her self-tan, she'll owe me. And I'll a have a pretty snappy riposte if she starts in on that shaggy bit about me cruising the Condé Nast building . . .* And I thought I could probably make her laugh at herself some-day—maybe later that afternoon in fact—highlighting the comedy of her blithe diva-tism. Can you call it *self*-tanning if you have to wake your husband to put the lotion on? And by now shouldn't self-tanners have evolved the ability to reach that recherché area between their shoulder blades on their own? Sure enough, Kate came around to the clown show of her monomania. Such forgivable outrages are the stuff of intimacy, transgressions that define the borders of the marriage and yet expand them too. The foundation of any union in some sense is the acknowledgment that we all have needs we are unequipped to meet alone. That some are more ludicrous than others is beside the point—the burden and pathos of need itself is the farce we've been assigned to enact. The sting of it is easier with a partner—easier to bear, easier to celebrate. Wa-kened from sleep to perform some ludicrous service for my wife, I'm obliged to acknowledge the ludicrous needs I have imposed on her—the defects of the social lummox, the blind mole who can't find the stapler, the keys, the apple juice, the Teletubby video. I'm obliged to remember that she once helped me get off Mt. Kiliman-jaro when my knee swelled up and I was unable to walk on my own. And of course because I married late and will likely grow ill or infirm before her, I'm obliged to remember the day will come when being able to vault out of bed to help my wife self-tan will seem like paradise.

What I understand now is that the mystery of why I waited so long to marry is no mystery at all. I can see the wisdom in that moment of wrenching sentimentality years ago. "First thought, best thought,"

Allen Ginsberg once said. The fate that crossed my path with Kate's would not be hurried. Our time is our time, and it takes what it takes. Where love comes from I have no idea, but I know we will look for the place together.

Incision

COLIN HARRISON

Promising until death did them part, Earl and Jean were married during Eisenhower's second term, and the Kodachrome slides taken on their wedding day on a colonial porch in Massachusetts show two stunning young people, dark-haired both, full of appetite for the future as well as for each other. Earl was a wizard with a tennis racquet, with broad shoulders and big hands and feet. He'd been born to replace an older sister, who had succumbed to a common childhood infection. His father had died of overwork a few years before. Having grown up with a depressed and anxious mother, and often visited by a lobotomized aunt, he'd chosen his wife for her basic good health, among other attributes. Jean was an aspiring actress, also from a good family, and smart enough for the both of them. She chose her husband in part because he had already confronted some of life's sorrows and carried himself with a quiet dignity. He was dependable, a man you could lean on, not that she planned to lean on anyone. Living in New York City, they would be mostly happy and almost poor. When they wanted to go to the movies, they dug around in the couch for loose change. They were young married people, and the curled photos that exist from that time show that they were slim and wore sunglasses and lay around in Central Park on Sunday afternoons reading the newspaper. If they had fears, which of course they did, then those fears existed in proper proportion to their happiness.

The decade rolled over; the marriage got bigger. Within a year they had a son—me—and less than two years later, another son. My father was practical yet also idealistic. He spoke well in public, listened carefully to others, and looked great in a white shirt and tie. He was also cheap and could not be trusted to buy a decent pair of shoes for himself. My mother cobbled together acting jobs, did a few commercials, stints on TV soap operas, which she detested. She was a dutiful yet distracted mother, not utterly devoted to the role—a situation that my father accepted. He himself worked too long each day, as his father had. By the end of the sixties, my parents were approaching forty—my father was still a wizard with a tennis racquet, but the skill was nearly extraneous within his big grown-up life. He was running a large, old country boarding school that was racked by drugs, intergenerational conflict, and the agony of Vietnam. My mother didn't have enough of the work she needed. Her dreams of acting had taken a hard backseat to his career. This was not easy on either of them; it simmered and sometimes boiled.

Still their marriage got bigger. It had to hold the boys, the work, the private conversations between a man and a woman. But this was not all. My mother's father, a robust sportsman whose charm and confidence were not so different from my father's, had been beaten down by colon surgery, heart attacks, and prostate cancer. He died gently and with no warning, carried away by the flu the same month that Nixon was sworn in for his second term. The loss of her father devastated my mother into speechlessness. She watched her own mother become a widow, hour by hour. And although my mother was pulled back into her days—she had teenaged sons to battle, groceries, the car—she shrank from her father's death, never grieved openly, never discussed it, in part because the end of his life meant she was older too and the vessel of her marriage now held death. She saw her mother's loneliness, the finality of it.

Through the tumbling decades, through Reagan and Bush and

Clinton, my parents' marriage kept changing, as marriages must do if they are to stay true; through the rise of my silver-haired father into genuine national prominence in his field, through the burial of his mother, the burial of my mother's mother, their sons in college, the first cracks of arthritis and forgetfulness, sons married, grandchildren arriving one by one. My parents' marriage will keep getting bigger whether either of them wants it to or not. My father is diagnosed with prostate cancer, having carefully avoided telling the doctor of his symptoms. Thinking with the confidence of an old jock, which my mother tells him was plain stupid. Years later she will not quite forgive him. Surgery is followed by radiation, which is followed by hormonal therapy. And strangely enough, it finally seems to work. His prostate cancer is statistically undetectable. My father retires to great acclaim at sixty-five. His school names the main building after him. Yet his retirement is a little pillowy and strange for them both, and between volunteer activities, they start taking trips. Their sons are more or less settled down. There's a lot to look back on now. She'd married the right man, she can say that. They hug in the kitchen, they work in the garden together. Now she is sixty-seven; now he is almost seventy, still a bit of a wizard with a tennis racquet. Somehow he has learned to peck away on the computer and manage the Internet. But friends are starting to die. The sons have gray hair now and talk passionately about their mortgages. She watches their marriages get bigger, as they must, to hold the work and children and conversation. There will be no more grandchildren, she senses. But that is not all that my mother senses, watching her husband pee too often. There is more. There is what she has always feared.

Which is where I will begin, or rather, continue. By this time, I was well past forty and my parents' marriage had become part of my own marriage, a story studied for its own sake but also as a referential text. How did my father deal with the demands of children and work? I wondered as I dealt with those same demands. How did my mother find patience for everyone, including herself? How did my parents discuss their parents? How did they watch their parents approach the end of life?

That last question began to pull at the edges of my day. My father didn't seem right. He was tired, aging before my eyes. My wife and I threw a big seventieth birthday party for him at a pricey resort. He put on a good face, and the grandchildren had a great time. But the trip to the resort had been a nightmare, my mother confessed to me. My father had something wrong with his bladder, a condition that was making him urinate half a dozen times an hour, so often that he did it even as he and I spoke on the phone each evening. And soon he was also having trouble with his bowels, a struggle about which he'd told me little—and yet quite enough for me to feel a rising fear.

The next spring, my parents visited from their home in Washington, D.C. I walked with my father to a bakery in our Brooklyn neighborhood. He made hearty banter with the salesgirl about the muffins and bread baked there, then turned to me and said in a low voice that he was tired and wanted to return to the house where my wife and I lived, only seven blocks away.

When my father and mother canceled their annual visit to us that summer, my wife suggested that I take the train from Manhattan to Washington to see him. We'd been looking forward to a long summer's weekend of tennis, swimming, and play. "You should go," my wife urged me, condemning herself to handling our three kids alone that weekend. "Something's going on."

When I arrived, my mother seemed to cling to me as we embraced. She was exhausted and worried. The diagnostic tests weren't producing a clear picture of what was afflicting my father. Yet it seemed impossible that the cluster of eminent physicians looking at him would not soon get on the proverbial same page—in this case updated and faxed to each of them by my mother—and administer some high-dollared expertise to fix up my father. In fact, although he seemed weak, distracted by pain, and six or eight pounds lighter, the gravity of the situation, the first awareness that we might be on a short clock, did not come to me until I accidentally encountered him that first night I visited.

As usual on my trips to my parents' house, I stayed up late flicking through their eighty cable-TV channels, achieving a kind of hypnotized oblivion. At about two A.M. I heard my father come down the stairs and got up to see him. He was standing in the kitchen, naked but for a diaper. I had known, in the abstract, that he'd started using diapers, but here was the actual thing, pale blue, oddly ruffled in the rear, his legs too skinny beneath them. His eyes lifted in dull consideration of my presence. I was surprised by the sight of him, diapered and thin, and I looked surprised. But my shock at his appearance seemed to be of no interest to him. If I was just waking up to the real truth of things, then it was about time. *I've hidden as much of this from you and your brother and your wives and children as long I can,* his slackened face seemed to say. *It's time to understand what the hell's really happening.* And anyway, my problems were not his concern. He had pills to take. OxyContin, to be exact. He seized the bottle like a man addicted, like a man terrified of what the pain would feel like if it reached him before the pills pushed it back. He needed those pills more than he needed to worry about my perception of reality, which, my father surely knew, would soon include the fact that he was dying.

That was in early August. Five weeks later, my father was hospitalized with complete kidney failure. His ureters, which would normally continuously convey urine from the kidneys to the bladder, were blocked. I got the call at my office, told my mother I'd be there as soon as possible. When I arrived at Sibley Memorial Hospital, my father was alive but weak. The doctors had performed an emergency nephrostomy, which meant they had catheterized his

209

kidneys from behind, right through his back, allowing the organs to begin draining. But there was another problem: my father's lower bowel was also blocked. He was scared and miserable and already tired of being in a bed. He asked that my mother rub his feet and legs with skin lotion. She did, as if it might help.

The following Monday, a crack surgeon decided to open my father up to see what was going on inside and perhaps remove the bowel blockage. He made a long incision that began below my father's breastbone and continued down around his navel to an inch above his gray pubic hair. Inside the surgeon saw cancer everywhere—bowel, kidneys, bladder. The pathology report would show that the cancer was an angiosarcoma—rare and always untreatable, and quite possibly caused by the very radiation treatment my father had received for his prostate cancer. The surgeon removed a large piece of the lower bowel and performed a colostomy to allow for the passage of waste. But beyond that there was nothing he could do, and he closed my father up.

How long? My mother could barely ask. They'd been together for fifty years.

Two months, the surgeon guessed.

He came home, losing weight steadily. My mother and brother moved him into the sunroom on the first floor where he could watch the garden from his rented hospital bed. My fall became a blur of train rides back and forth from New York to Washington. Each time, I tried to work on the train but lapsed into distracted contemplation of the beautiful foliage flashing by. I would go down on Friday and stay until Monday. My wife would go down on Monday and stay until Friday. To do this she zeroed out her calendar, canceling every professional event she had scheduled, including ones abroad that had been planned for more than a year. The shared running of the family was now accomplished at night with one of us on the phone from our home, the other having just walked away from my father's bedside, where the nurse had taken over the stroking of his hand (the wedding ring newly loose on his finger) or now bent close to his anguished face to listen for his whispered request. Our marriage was getting bigger; each of us knew that the other was having an experience that had not yet been talked about or understood, an experience that was like the other's and yet different, separate. There was mystery in this. I had never been with my wife as we watched someone we loved die day by day. We were masked by sadness, even to each other. And although it was my father who was dying, not my wife's, her grief was no less deeply felt, it seemed to me, and in my own private way I studied my wife's sorrow so that I might somehow understand my own.

In these comings and goings, my wife and I sometimes overlapped in Washington for a few hours or even a night. One of those mornings I woke and found my way downstairs where she had spent the night with my father. When I stepped into the sunroom, I saw my wife rubbing his feet and legs in one long motion, not unlike a rower leaning into her stroke and pulling hard all the way back. Her eyes were closed as she pushed her hands along the length of his long, shrunken feet and then up his shins, nearly reaching his knees. He was asleep or at least adrift in his twilight world.

She opened her eyes and appeared both fatigued and at peace. "You did this the whole night?" I asked. "Rubbed his feet?"

"Well," she said, "he liked it."

"Come get some breakfast."

"In a minute."

With that my father stirred and opened his eyes enough for me to know that he'd heard the conversation at the foot of his bed.

"I'm tough competition," he whispered with a smile, his mouth dry. Then he lapsed backward and I knew that my wife's devotion to him through the night had both relieved his pain and brought him reassurance—that he was not alone, that someone was touching him, that the solitary rower soothing her hands over his feet and legs hundreds of times each hour was not acting out of charity but passion. Though I loved my father deeply, without reservation, I knew I was not capable of this same act, and even if I were capable of it, I doubt it would have been received with the same satisfaction.

My father's deep belly incision from the failed exploratory surgery became infected and had to be opened up, cleaned, and left open to heal from the inside out. But as the weeks went by, the healing slowed and the two sides did not meet and bind up. The hospice-care nurses dutifully changed the dressing on the incision each day. Thus my father now had four unnatural openings in his abdomen: the unhealing surgical wound, usually covered by pads of gauze kept in place by translucent tape; the smaller hole that emptied his bowels into his colostomy bag, and the two pencil-thick nephro-stomy holes that allowed direct tube-drainage of his kidneys into two bags hung on either side of his bed. My wife often witnessed the cleansing and care of these openings into my father's flesh, and though she winced in sadness while describing them to me, neither did she shield herself from seeing them or in any other way pretend that they were not there.

I, on the other hand, was quite fearful of those four holes. Although my father lay before me wasted by pain, he appeared nonetheless complete—but for those openings, which seemed the most objective proof of the destruction occurring within him. Or not just the proof but the *portals* to that destruction, the way toward the furnace of cancer inside him and its way toward me. I counted my unwillingness to look directly at those four holes as rank cowardice on my part, a pathetic inability to deal with the plain truth. "I want you to see this thing *through*," my father once said to me from his bed, and although there were a number of interpretations of that statement (including being sure that we did not cruelly extend his life), all of them included the necessity that I deal directly with his bodily reality. So here he was dying in his bed, here were my mother and her sister, and my brother and his wife, and other relatives, all waiting on my father, here were the nurses tenderly lifting and adjusting, feeding and wiping, and here too again was my wife alongside them. I did what I could, stroking my father's forehead, feeding him ice chips, wetting his lips, and, when he whispered *okay* and squeezed my hand, pressing the button on the electronic device that delivered a bolus of Dilaudid, a synthetic morphine, into his bloodstream. But when it came time to roll my father over so that his backside could be cleaned or rubbed, I avoided seeing the place where the two thin kidney catheters disappeared into his back. *You are a fucking miserable coward,* I told myself.

My father and I had always been very physical with each other—wrestling, bumping hard in basketball, tackling in the living room—and one morning I felt the desire to hold him, to feel his weight, which of course was now impossible. But somehow this wish for physical intimacy became my ability to at last gaze upon the catheters. They were not as disturbing as I'd expected, and a little while later I watched the colostomy bag as it was being changed. This was shocking—there was my father's yellowy brown waste, held in a clear plastic pouch—yet there was something comforting in the notion that these three unnatural orifices were meant to duplicate their respective natural ones, that they had a helpful function, to carry away the dead cells and waste of a dying body.

But I had not yet seen the central wound into my father's torso, the dark, vertical sword-cut hidden beneath gauze and tape. I feared this wound, feared what it meant, feared its power to wound me.

"It's very deep," my wife said one night. "It's shocking."

"I haven't seen it yet," I confessed.

"I know," she said with kindness.

"I think I should see it," I went on, scarcely believing myself. "It's there, it's part of the reality."

My wife fixed her eyes on mine, her face still, mouth closed. In this expression her strong cheekbones are particularly apparent, as is too her years of toil, with her children, her work, herself. And with me, of course. She has a touch of Cherokee blood in her—mixed up with all sorts of other heritages—and the face she showed me reminded me of the daguerreotypes of great Indian chiefs who knew nature and death intimately.

"No," she finally said. "I don't think you should see it."

I was surprised. "No?"

"I don't think it's a good idea."

Her statement held no superiority or judgment, just wisdom about her husband's ability to witness his father's death. About what was grief and what was horror. *It will do no one any good for you to gaze into the shadowy red blackness of the wound inside your father that will never heal,* she was saying. *It will distract from the difficulties already at hand. It will fuck you up.*

Her opposition was as forceful as a hand pressed against my chest. Nonetheless, I began, "Well, I should just look—"

"It's the most terrible thing I've ever seen," my wife said. She was not given to hyperbole, especially in relation to her own experience, and so to call the incision the most terrible meant that it was worse than the sight of her own mother's bedsores, open to the bone; worse than the sight of her grandfather after his leg was amputated at age ninety-two. I'd chosen her as a wife in part because she had already confronted some of life's sorrows. Yes, the worst ever for my wife was very bad, worse even than seeing our oldest daughter struck with pneumonia when only six days old; worse than the time at age nine her blood suddenly stopped clotting and her legs turned purple and swollen—making the emergency-ward doctor mutter that this was what the onset of leukemia looked like; worse than the sight of our son knocked limply unconscious from a fall at age two;

214

worse than the sight of him at age ten in the ICU pumped full of steroids and breathing oxygen after a severe onset of asthma. Each of these things had deeply traumatized my wife, and it occurred to me that not only did she not want me to see the wound, she wanted at least one of us not to have seen it.

"Okay," I said, "I guess I won't."

The unhealed incision thus became a kind of vortex; my wife's consciousness had been inside it and mine had not, except by way of my own imagination.

As my father failed, he said less and less. He needed to conserve his energy and he was also making an interior journey of preparation. I knew that when he was awake, he was thinking. We all knew it. We knew it because he would often open his eyes and say one or two words that fit perfectly into the conversation around him. I also knew he was thinking because he told me so, saying at one point, "I'm learning a great deal about time and consciousness."

As death approached, he did not ruminate or complain about his suffering. Whereas he had once studied his incision when it was being cleaned, now it did not interest him. He did not say much beyond *Thank you* and *Please*. But the pain was mounting as the cancer spread. There was an asymmetrical mass in his abdomen, a strange white spot on the roof of his mouth. His right eye appeared to be drying up. With the pain came higher and higher doses of Dilaudid, and he lapsed into a kind of earnestness that was both childlike and hallucinatory.

At 5:02 P.M. one afternoon, he said to me, "May I please go home?"

"Yes," I said.

"May I go?" he asked again.

"Yes."

"Thank you."

215

At 5:05 P.M. he said, "Please don't take me home."

I nodded my assent.

At 5:10 P.M. he whispered, "Take me home . . . too much pain."

Three days later my mother did take him home, in the most difficult, most loving act of her life. Together with her sister, who had lost her own husband to cancer decades earlier, and a nurse, she held my father as she took him home. Many times in the last thirty years I have not been particularly charitable toward my mother, but I recognize that her strength on this night completely surpassed my understanding of her and the nature of her love for my father. And yet, it was not surprising at all. She had never faltered in her care for him, not once. She had exhausted all of herself for him, had emptied any and everything she could give into him. She had in the near hours to his death called him "such a beautiful man, the most beautiful man." She loved him with all her heart, and she did what he needed, what he had asked for, and what was best.

I had said good-bye the previous afternoon in Washington, knowing it was the last time I might see my father, and, having not taken the train this one time, somehow drove the first fifty miles while weeping. Back in New York, my wife and I lay in our marriage bed knowing that he would probably die that night. If we said anything, I cannot remember what it was. I suspect we just lay there, knowing, waiting for the call. It came.

Not long ago, five months after my father's memorial service, my wife and I were remembering him one evening as we sat on our favorite couch. Our children lay asleep. The conversation turned toward the unhealed incision. My wife's insistence that I not see it came back to me, seemed all the more wise. That I had not seen it had spared me, of course, but it meant that the symbiotic intelligence of our marriage, the joint brain, had both ingested the knowledge of the wound, been wounded by the wound, and yet included someone who had escaped its worst trauma.

"It might have taken greater strength not to look," my wife said.

This surprised me; I didn't understand.

"To not look requires a kind of faith that I might not have," my wife admitted. "That incision is with me every day . . . a little part of my day disappears into that hole."

"Maybe you looked at it so that I wouldn't," I said.

Maybe. Maybe anything. We didn't have any answers, any useful perception. She had looked into the incision, I had not. Neither decision had affected the outcome. We would miss my father forever. We'd put pictures of him everywhere. My wife dreamed of him constantly, whereas I had glimpsed him just once while asleep. He'd been smiling. Later I had stared at a box of family videotapes, which held many minutes of him at Christmases and Thanksgivings and birthdays. I couldn't watch them, not now anyway. His death was fresh and deep and healing only slowly. It might never heal completely. We would both have to care for the wound together, in ourselves and in each other.

"Oh, why do we have to die?" my wife cried now, carried by her thoughts.

We sat there then, on the couch, children asleep in their beds, ours awaiting us. There was no need to say aloud what we both feared—that one of us would die first. The other would somehow see the thing through, as had my mother, whose own death would someday come. But there was a worse fear—I can barely bring myself to write these words—that one of our children could die before we did. Or one of their children. And even if those most terrible things never happened, then surely older family and friends would die before we did.

All this was known long before it would be understood. But with my father's death, the first one very close to me, the first one my wife and I had experienced together, came our deeper awareness that now, in our forties, we had probably reached that moment when the vessel of our marriage held not just love and children and work but was beginning to fill slowly with death as well.

ACKNOWLEDGMENTS

The editors of this anthology would like to express their profound gratitude to the contributors, men who agreed to open personal lives to scrutiny for the sake of this project. Without their candor and generosity: no book. Thanks also to Colin Dickerman, Stephen Morrison, and Marisa Pagano at Bloomsbury and Billy Kingsland, John Bennett, and Corby Hawks at Kuhn Projects. We are especially grateful to Chip Kidd for producing a magnificent cover on a tight deadline. Individually, David Kuhn would like to thank Kevin Thompson for being committed and Belle and Roger Kuhn for having been committed for nearly fifty years. Chris Knutsen would like to thank Nuar, who never lets the fragile sequence break, and Isadora, for bringing all joy. Every day, they are the light and the way, the measure of all commitment.

ABOUT THE CONTRIBUTORS

Louis Begley has written seven novels: *Shipwreck* (2003), *Schmidt Delivered* (2000), *Mistlers's Exit* (1998), *About Schmidt* (1996), *As Max Saw It* (1994), *The Man Who Was Late* (1993), and *Wartime Lies* (1991). He has received, among other prizes, the PEN/Ernest Hemingway Foundation fiction award, an American Academy of Acts are Letters Award in Literature, and the Prix Médicis Étranger, for *Wartime Lies*. Until his retirement in 2004, Begley was a senior partner at the law firm Debevoise & Plimpton, and the head of its international practice. He is married to Anka Muhlstein, the prize-winning French author of biographies and other historical works. They live in New York City.

Andy Borowitz is the author of several humor books, including *Who Moved My Soap?: The CEO's Guide to Surviving in Prison* (2003) and *The Trillionaire Next Door: The Greedy Investor's Guide to Day Trading* (2000), which was a finalist for the 2001 Thurber Prize. His most recent book, *The Borowitz Report: The Big Book of Shockers* (2004), is based on his humor Web site, BorowitzReport .com, which has millions of readers around the world. His humor pieces appear regularly in the *New Yorker*, the *New York Times*, *Vanity Fair*, and at Newsweek.com. An actor and comedian, Borowitz appears on CNN's *American Morning* and in the Woody Allen film *Melinda and Melinda* (2004). In July 2004 Borowitz won the National Press Club's first-ever award for humor.

Chip Brown, a contributing editor for *Men's Journal,* is the author of two nonfiction books, *Good Morning Midnight: Life and Death* *in the* Wild (2003) and *Afterwards, You're a Genius: Faith, Medicine, and the Metaphysics of Healing* (2000). From 1979 to 1985 he was a staff writer with the *Washington Post,* and Brown has also been a contributing editor for *Esquire* and a correspondent for *Outside.* His work has appeared in the *New York Times Magazine,* the *New Yorker, Harper's, Vanity Fair, Vogue, GQ, Condé Nast Traveler,* and *National Geographic Adventure,* among other magazines. In 1989, Brown won the National Magazine Award for feature writing. He is married to writer and editor Kate Betts. They live in New York City with their five-year-old son, Oliver.

Rich Cohen is the author of a memoir, *Lake Effect* (2002), as well as the nonfiction books *Machers and Rockers: Chess Records and the Birth of Rock 'n' Roll* (2004), *The Avengers* (2000), and *Tough Jews* (1998). His work has appeared in the *New Yorker* and *Vanity Fair,* among other publications. He is a contributing editor for *Rolling Stone.* He lives in New York City with his wife, Jessica, and their newborn son, Aaron.

Geoff Dyer is the author of the novels *Paris Trance* (1998), *The Search* (1993), and *The Colour of Memory* (1989). His nonfiction books include *The Ongoing Moment* (2005), *Yoga for People Who Can't Be Bothered to Do It* (2004), *Anglo-English Attitudes* (1999), *Out of Sheer Rage* (1997), *But Beautiful* (1996), and *The Missing of the Somme* (1994). He received the Somerset Maugham Award for *But Beautiful,* was short-listed for the National Book Critics Circle Award for *Out of Sheer Rage,* and, in 2003, was awarded a Literary Fellowship by the Lannan Foundation.

Tad Friend has been a staff writer at the *New Yorker* since 1998 and now writes its "Letter from California." His recent book, *Lost in Magnolia: Travels in Hollywood and Other Foreign Lands* (2001), is a collection of essays and reporting on an array of cultural topics. His writing has been featured in *The Best American Sports Writing* and *The Best American Travel Writing*. He lives with his wife, *New York Times* food columnist Amanda Hesser, in Brooklyn.

David Grand has written the novels *The Disappearing Body* (2002) and *Louse* (1998). He currently lives in Brooklyn with his wife, Christine, and their twin sons.

Colin Harrison is a senior editor at Scribner and was formerly the deputy editor of *Harper's*. He is the author of five novels: *The Havana Room* (2004), *Afterburn* (2000), *Manhattan Nocturne* (1996), *Bodies Electric* (1993), and *Break and Enter* (1990). He lives in Brooklyn with his wife, the writer Kathryn Harrison.

Jay McInerney is the author of the novels *Model Behavior* (1998), *The Last of the Savages* (1996), *Brightness Falls* (1992), *Story of My Life* (1988), *Ransom* (1985), and *Bright Lights, Big City* (1984), which he also adapted for film. His recent book, *Bacchus and Me: Adventures in the Wine Cellar* (2002), is a collection of his wine columns from *House and Garden* magazine. His fiction has appeared in *Esquire,* the *Paris Review,* and the *Atlantic Monthly*. He lives in New York City.

Jonathan Mahler is a contributing writer to the *New York Times Magazine*. His first book is *Ladies and Gentlemen, the Bronx Is Burning* (2005). He lives in Brooklyn with his wife, *New York Times* editor Danielle Mattoon, and their son, Gus.

James McManus is the author of the books *Positively Fifth Street: Murderers, Cheetahs, and Binion's World Series of Poker* (2003), *Going to the Sun* (1996), *Ghost Waves* (1988), and *Curtains* (1986). *Going to the Sun* received the Carl Sandburg Award, and in 2001,

McManus received the Peter Lisagor Award for sports journalism. McManus's work has appeared in *Harper's, Esquire, The Best American Poetry, The Best American Sports Writing,* the *New York Times,* and on NPR's *This American Life.* He lives with his wife, Jennifer, and their daughters near Chicago, where he teaches writing and comparative literature at the School of the Art Institute.

Rick Moody is the author of the novels *The Black Veil* (2002), *Purple America* (1997), *The Ice Storm* (1994), and *Garden State* (1991), which won the Pushcart Press Editor's Choice Award. He has also written two collections of short fiction, *Demonology* (2001) and *The Ring of Brightest Angels Around Heaven: A Novella and Stories* (1995). He was coeditor of *Joyful Noise: The New Testament Revisited* (1997). In 2003 *The Black Veil* was awarded the Martha Albrand Award from PEN American Center. Other awards include a Guggenheim Fellowship, an Addison Metcalf Award, and an Aga Khan Prize. His fiction and essays have appeared in the *New Yorker, Esquire,* the *Paris Review, Harper's, Grand Street, Details,* the *New York Times,* and *The Believer.* Moody, who was married last May to Amy Osborn, divides his time between Fishers Island and Brooklyn, New York.

David Owen is a staff writer for the *New Yorker.* He is the author of a dozen books, among them *Copies in Seconds* (2004), *The Chosen One* (2001), and *My Usual Game* (1995). He lives in northwest Connecticut with his wife, the writer Ann Hodgman, and their two children.

John Burnham Schwartz is the author of the novels *Claire Marvel* (2002), *Reservation Road* (1998), and *Bicycle Days* (1989). His work has appeared in the *New York Times,* the *New Yorker,* the *Boston Globe, Vogue, Doubletake,* and *Newsday.* In 1991, Schwartz received the Lyndhurst Foundation Award. Currently, he is the deputy director of the Sun Valley Writers' Conference. He lives in Brooklyn with his wife, Aleksandra Crapanzano.

John Seabrook is the author of *Nobrow: The Culture of Marketing, the Marketing of Culture* (2000) and *Deeper: My Two-Year Odyssey in Cyberspace* (1997). He has been a staff writer at the *New Yorker* since 1993, and his work has also appeared in *Harper's*, the *Nation, Vanity Fair, Vogue, Travel + Leisure,* and the *Village Voice.* He has taught narrative nonfiction writing at Princeton University. Seabrook lives in Rome with his wife, the writer Lisa Reed, and their son.

David Sedaris is the author of the collections *Dress Your Family in Corduroy and Denim* (2004), *Me Talk Pretty One Day* (2000), *Naked* (1997), *Holidays on Ice* (1997), and *Barrel Fever* (1994). He is a regular contributor to the *New Yorker, GQ,* and NPR's *This American Life.* He and his boyfriend, Hugh Hamrick, curently live in London.

Nicholas Weinstock's writing has been featured on National Public Radio and in the *New York Times Magazine,* the *Nation, Vogue, Glamour, Ladies' Home Journal, Out, Poets & Writers* and other publications. He is the author of the novels *The Golden Hour* (2005) and *As Long as She Needs Me* (2001), and the nonfiction book *The Secret Love of Sons* (1997). Weinstock is director of comedy development for 20th Century Fox Television. He lives in Los Angeles with his wife, Amanda Beesley, and their children.

James Wolcott is the author of *Attack Poodles and Other Media Mutants: The Looting of the News in a Time of Terror* (2004) and *The Catsitters: A Novel* (2001). He is the cultural critic for *Vanity Fair* and has been a staff writer at the *Village Voice, Esquire, Harper's,* and the *New Yorker.* He and his wife, the writer Laura Jacobs, live in New York City.

A NOTE ON THE EDITORS

Chris Knutsen is an articles editor at *GQ*. Formerly, he worked at Riverhead Books and the *New Yorker*.

David Kuhn is the founder of Kuhn Projects, a book packaging company and literary agency in New York City. He has been the editor in chief of *Brill's Content*, executive editor of *Talk*, features director of the *New Yorker,* and a senior editor at *Vanity Fair*.

A NOTE ON THE TYPE

The text of this book is set in Linotype Sabon, named after the type founder Jacques Sabon. It was designed by Jan Tschichold and jointly developed by Linotype, Monotype, and Stempel, in response to a need for a typeface to be available in identical form for mechanical hot metal composition and hand composition using foundry type.

Tschichold based his design for Sabon roman on a font engraved by Garamond, and Sabon italic on a font by Granjon. It was first used in 1966 and has proved an enduring modern classic.